Song of the Ground Jay

To my grandmothers,
Tahereh and Zinat

to my mother,
Ezzat

and
to my daughter,
Tina

CONTENTS

INTRODUCTION

About the Selection

The past century has witnessed a marked increase in the number of Iranian women as literary critics, authors, playwrights and poets. Some recent anthologies include more than three hundred women poets born in the last century. This compilation includes one hundred women poets born after September 1941, which spans the reign of Mohammad Reza Shah Pahlavi and the Islamic Republic, arguably the most progressive period for women's rights and the most regressive and restrictive period for Iranian women respectively.

Choosing a select few was not an easy task. I started with a list of over three hundred poets. I read several poems by each. I chose those whose poetry I most appreciated and searched for additional poems by the selected poets. Once I chose the poets, I further limited my scope by considering accessibility, content and form. I eliminated those who had most of their poems already translated to English, as those poems were already accessible to anglophones.

Further narrowing the selection, I eliminated those poems that were heavily contextualized: poems whose themes lent themselves to great literary criticism for, among other things, their deep roots in social, historical, national or religious traditions. These elements, though valuable, may not be universally appreciated.

A handful of poets, such as Samaneh Kahrobaeian and Fatemeh Salarvand, in this collection write ghazals (sonnets/odes), a form of classical Persian poetry of five to fourteen lines, the first line rhyming with the even lines. Another group writes in the classical form of robai'i or do-beiti (couplet). Most of the poets in this collection, however, write in the free verse style that started to be used after 1920.

As to form, if a poet has both classical and modern poems, I have chosen the modern poems. In most cases, I have chosen the shorter poems. My choices of poets and their respective poems were guided primarily by my heart. I needed a personal connection to the poem before I could take on its translation. As a result, you may find little known poets in this collection. Conversely, some poets that have appeared in other anthologies, may not appear here. This compilation represents a collection of poems whose essence I related to and could convey through translation. A handful of these poems have been translated by others, though may not have been published. Some of the original poems have not appeared in a book before.

The Genesis & the Compulsion

Looking back at my notebooks, in every list since 2015 there is an entry about women and poetry ranging from: recite poetry by women and upload to social media, look into the poetry of women about being a woman to questions such as "I wonder how many contemporary Persian women poets we have?"

In 2020, I met two Iranian poets at a virtual class about contemporary Persian poetry by women. Their approach to poetry was delightful, their presence moving. Their poetry connected past literary traditions to current literary themes. As they recited their poems tears streamed down my face. They were not tears of sadness, but rather a re-establishment of a dormant connection. It's similar to reconnecting with a close relative or friend who lives far away and when you get the chance to reconnect you realize how many cherished memories you had but had since forgotten. It's an overwhelming feeling.

I had to do something with that experience. I was on a mission to introduce these poets to English speakers, especially to second generation Iranians who may not know Persian well enough to appreciate poetry. Through this project, I learned about what it means to be passionate and to feel you are on a mission in a way I had not experienced before. I spent nights and early mornings on it. I was perfectly fine forgoing social commitments, gatherings, and sleep to complete this project. The book had permeated every aspect of my life. Every conversation with my daughter was peppered with progress on the project or asking her to choose between two words in a line. When I was searching for a title, I had responded to my partner's very kind greeting on a Sunday morning with "Do you know that there are only two birds endemic to Iran?" While I saw nothing wrong with this, he (and everyone who has heard the story) seemed to disagree!

What you are reading is the result. My hope is that the poems will resonate with you, that you will appreciate the situation of women in Iran and celebrate their strength and resilience.

About the Title

Iranian Ground Jay (*Podoces pleskei*) is a bird from the crow family endemic to Iran. It lives in the desert and its coloring is perfectly adapted to its habitat, allowing it to blend in. Though it is sand colored when on the ground, when in flight it has beautiful black and white wingtips. One of its distinguishing features is its strong and muscular legs, enabling it to walk and run long distances. Its beautiful song distinguishes it from other members of the crow family.

To me it is a powerful symbol of survival, the ability to at once adapt to one's environment and distinguish oneself through song and strength…in short it is a symbol of Iranian women. Interestingly, in 2021 a new postal stamp commemorated the Iranian ground jay.

About the Structure of this Anthology

In the short biographies of the poets, you will sometimes encounter an empty gray frame for the photo or [—]. These indicate that either the photo or information was not available to me, or that the poet has asked that some details not be included. I have also sometimes included photos that were not of very high quality because I think that even a somewhat pixelated photo is better than none.

For the books field, I have only included the poet's poetry collections published in Persian. If a poet has novels, books of literary criticism, etc., they have not been included.

At the end of each poem I have placed a branch 🌿 to indicate the end of the poem; and for the final poem of a poet's work in this collection I have indicated it with an acorn 🌰.

Acknowledgments

I am indebted to so many people who helped me complete this project. My daughter Tina who is my first reader, kindest critic, and a constant source of love and encouragement. She has enriched the translations through inquiry, attention to detail, thoughtful comments and her ability to address any and all linguistic and technological challenges. My friend Debbie Rusch, who read the manuscript and provided candid feedback and much needed humor. My aunt, Najmieh Batmanglij, who has taught me about passion and purpose in life and encouraged my pursuit of what is meaningful to me, including this project. My friend, Sayeh Eghtesadinia, who has been a great resource; serving as a connector, trusted advisor, and cheerleader. My partner Arjang Assad, whose remarkable vocabulary, love, patience and sense of humor transformed each word choice into a delightful exchange.

I met Farideh Hassanzadeh, Kamyar Abedi and Soheila Mirzaei through this project. These new connections were some of the most unexpected and delightful parts of my work. Among other acts of kindness, they helped connect me to others.

I consider myself incredibly lucky when it comes to women role models. This book is dedicated to my mother Ezzat, to the memory of my grandmothers, Zinat and Tahereh, and to my daughter Tina, my hope for the future.

Song of the Ground Jay

Poems by Iranian Women, 1960–2022

Rira Abbasi

Date of Birth: 1962

Place of Birth: Khorramabad

Place of Residence: England

Education: [—]

Profession: peace poet, author & founder and director of the
International Festival of Peace Poetry in Iran

Books: five poetry collections

به امیدواری سری می‌زنم
از هر کسی بیش‌تر صدا می‌زنم
ری‌را، ری‌را
فراموش می‌کنم جهان در ستیز است
دوباره از صلح می‌گویم
تا بیش‌تر فراموشم کنند

૭

I drop in on hope
More than anyone, I call out
Rira, Rira*
I forget the world is at war
I speak of peace again
So they will forget me more

⚘

---

* The poet's first name

خودشیفته‌ام
ببین
همیشه پیروزم
تاس می‌ریزم
که تاس بریزم
سفید، سیاه
تنهای تنها بازی می‌کنم

❧

اشتباه می‌کنم
دوباره به صورتم اشتباه می‌پاشم
بینی‌ام قرمز
زیر چشم‌هایم شور
گم‌شده در اتاقی قرمز
نمک
طعم این اشتباه می‌دهد
دوباره عشق را به صورتم می‌کشم

I am a narcissist
Look
I always win
I roll the dice
to roll the dice
White, black
I play all by myself.

I make a mistake
Again, I splash mistakes on my face
My nose red
Under my eyes salty
Lost in a red room
Salt
tastes like this mistake
Again I pull love over my face

Mana Aghaee

Date of Birth: 1973
Place of Birth: Bushehr
Place of Residence: Sweden
Education: MA, Iranian Languages, Uppsala University
Profession: translator, researcher and poet
Books: five poetry collections

آگهی همسریابی

زنی هستم بیست و هشت ساله
با عادت‌هایی غریب
و اشتباهاتی هم‌قد خودم
که صبح تا صبح دندان‌هایم را مسواک می‌زنم
پشت میز اداره می‌نشینم
و غصه‌هایم را
با خواندن «نیازمندی‌ها»ی روزنامه فراموش می‌کنم

من از توفان‌های بسیاری گذشته‌ام
من به حقوق همه‌ی حیوانات — حتی بشر — احترام می‌گذارم

Personal Ad (seeking husband)

I am a twenty-eight-year-old woman
with strange habits
Mistakes as large as life
I brush my teeth every morning
I sit at my desk at work
And I drown my sorrows by reading the classifieds

I have survived many storms
I respect the rights of all animals, even humans

من زجر کشیدن در راه یک هدف را
به لذت‌های زودگذر ترجیح می‌دهم
سینما را تحریم کرده‌ام
دامن‌های تنگ و پاشنه‌های بلند
حق آزادانه فکر کردن را از آدم می‌گیرند

خدای من مهربان است
او جهنم را برای عذاب وجدانم
و ویاگرا را برای بقای نسلم آفریده
من آدم بودن را با همه‌ی مضراتش پذیرفته‌ام
در این دنیایی که از هر گوشه‌ی سقفش
بمب شیمیایی چکه می‌کند
آدم باید احمق باشد که آرزوی فرشته شدن کند
و به زخم شانه‌هایش بال بدوزد

مردی که دنبالش می‌گردم
باید شریک اعتقاداتم باشد
او نباید در کتاب‌ها زندگی کند
و صورتش را برای هر ابرقدرتی جلو بیاورد
برای او دو شرط گذاشته‌ام:
اول اینکه هیچ وقت از رفتن خسته نشود
دوم اینکه فقط از کفش‌هایش اطاعت کند

and I favor suffering to achieve a goal
to the short-lived pleasures of life
I have boycotted the cinema
Tight skirts and high heels
As they rob me of my ability to think freely

My God is merciful
He has created hell to make me feel guilty
and Viagra for the survival of my species
I have accepted being human with all its perils
In a world where in its every corner a chemical
    bomb leaks
One would be foolish to wish to become an angel
To sew wings to the wounds on one's shoulder

The man I am looking for
Must share my beliefs
Must not have his nose buried in books
Must not turn the other cheek to every superpower
I have two conditions for him:
First, he should never tire of moving
Second, he should obey only his shoes.

زمستان معشوق من است

زمستان معشوق من است
مردی که حافظه ای سفید دارد
وَ گردنِ بلندش را
با غرور بالا می گیرد
زیر برف ها به قوی زیبایی می ماند
که روی دریاچه ی یخ زده ای می رقصد
در آغوشش می کشم
آب می شود
کم کم
کم کم آب می شود
وَ می ریزد
انگار هیچوقت نبوده
مردِ مهاجری که قرار بود گرمم کند.

❧

من و گنجشک‌ها

آوازی حزین خواند
بر شاخه های لاغر انگشتانم
پرید و رفت
حتی گنجشک هم دل نمی بندد
به زنی که مشتش پیش باد باز است

❧

Winter Is My Beloved

Winter is my beloved
A man with a white memory
And a tall neck
held up high with pride
Under the snow, he resembles a beautiful swan
Dancing on a frozen lake
I embrace him
he melts
Slowly, slowly
Slowly slowly he melts
and flows
As if he never existed
An immigrant who was supposed to warm me up.

❧

The Sparrows and I

It sang a sad song
On the thin branches of my fingers
It then flew away
Not even the sparrow
Will love
A woman
Whose secrets are open to the wind.

❧

ردّ پا

دنیا سفره‌ی هفت سین بود
زندگی تنگ بلور

نشستم و زل زدم
به ردّ پای ماهی‌هایی
که تبخیر شده بودند

~

شاعر شدم

شبی که ماه
در چاه فراموشی افتاده بود
— خیلی آسان —
طناب نازک خیالم را پایین انداختم
و او را بیرونش کشیدم.

Trails

The world was a New Year Setting*
Life, a glass decanter

I sat and stared
At the fish trails
That had evaporated

❧

Poet

I became a poet on a night
when the moon
Had fallen in the well of oblivion
 – very easily –
I threw the thin rope of my imagination to it
and pulled it out.

❧

---

* *haft seen* -the poet uses *haft seen* which I have translated to a
"New Year Setting," a setting arranged for the Persian New Year.
It contains seven (*haft*) symbols starting with the Persian letter
which is the phonetic equivalent of "s"(*seen*). In addition, there
is always a container with a live goldfish symbolizing life. Pisces
is also the twelfth and last astrological sign – end of year.

Asieh Amini

Date of Birth: 1973

Place of Birth: Ramsar

Place of Residence: Norway

Education: MA Cultural Studies (Diversity and Equality),
  Norwegian University of Science and Technology; BA,
  Communications with a journalism concentration, Allameh
  Tabatabae'i University

Profession: journalist, women's rights' activist, poet

Books: Three collections of poetry

گیرم که خدا مردی باشد
و من زنی
اگر عاشقش شوم...
چگونه در آغوشش بگیرم؟
کجا ببوسمش؟
چگونه دست در دستش بپیچم؟

Suppose God is a man
and I am a woman
If I fall in love with him...
How do I embrace him?
Where do I kiss him?
How do our hands intertwine?

بازوان او ابر أست یا صخره؟
و ساقدوش ما
کدام پیامبر اولی العزم خواهد بود؟

چه سقفی، کدام دیوار
عشقمان را در پناه می گیرد؟
بسترمان
در خونریز کدام شفق پهن می شود؟
وراستی
کودك ما
شکل کدام سرزمین جنگ زده خواهد بود؟

❧

ای دکه های مطبوعاتی
از این پس
جای روزنامه، سیگار
بفروشید
سیگار
هم گران تر است
هم برگشتی ندارد
هم هرگز کسی شما را
به خاطر انتشار دود
مجازات نخواهد کرد

His arms, are they clouds or rocks?
And which prophet
Will be our best man?

Which ceiling, which wall
will shelter our love?
On which twilight
will our bed be spread?
Incidentally
which war-torn land
will our child resemble?

§

Newsstands!
From now on
Instead of newspapers,
Sell cigarettes

For cigarettes
are more expensive
they cannot be returned
and nobody will ever punish you
for spreading smoke!

Farinaz Aryanfar

Date of Birth: 1984

Place of Birth: Tehran

Place of Residence: Sweden

Education: MS, Global Conflict Studies, Gothenburg
   University; BA Middle Eastern Studies, Leiden University

Profession: humanitarian project coordinator, socio-political
   analyst, poet

Books: one poetry collection

وجدان درد

دردناک بود
مردی که روی زمین نشسته بود
و به ستونی تکیه کرده بود
و با چشمان قهوه ای رنگش
به دوردستها مینگریست
دردناکتر بود
عابرانی که از کنارش می گذشتند
کسی نمی پرسید:
آقا کاری از من ساخته است
آقا اتفاقی افتاده است

The Conscience of Pain

It was painful
The man seated on the floor
Leaning on a pillar
With his brown eyes
Staring at a distance.
It was more painful
That passersby would walk by him
Nobody would ask
Man, is there anything I can do?
Has something happened?

فقط از کنارش عبور می کردند
حتی نگاهش نمی کردند
...
با خودت فکر نکن که شاید
من به سراغش رفتم
و حالش را جویا شدم
دردناکترین این بود
که من نیز
چون تمامی عابران
فقط از کنارش گذشتم

۶

نشانی

چه سوال عجیبی!
«نشانی قلبم!؟»
دستم را می برم به چانه ام
و میگویم:
نور نگاهم را که دنبال کردی
و به مهر لبخندم که رسیدی
دریچه ی احساساتم را می بوسی
و از پوست خاموشم عبور میکنی
با شیرین زبانی وارد رگهایم می شوی
همراه جریان خونم می روی
و می روی
و می روی
آنگاه

They would only walk by him
They would not even look at him
…
Don't believe that maybe I
Went to him
To ask how he was
It was most painful
That I
Like all other passersby
Just walked by him

Directions

What a strange question!
"Directions to my heart?"
I put my hand on my chin
And I say:
After following the light of my eyes
And after reaching my kind smile
You kiss the doorway to my feelings
And pass through my silent skin
With your sweet talk you enter my veins
You flow with my blood
And keep going
And going
Then

به مزرعه ی احساساتم
— قلبم —
می رسی
می رسی!
نقشه ی زخمهایم را می توانی مرور کنی
و بیاموزی:
بدون چتر نجات پریدن
لذتبار
و نیز دردناک است.
اکنون تو به مقصد رسیده ای
پس در کوچه های شلوغ عاطفه ام
می دوی.
ناگاه
بر میخوری به اثر انگشتانت
که بر دیواره های قلبم
خط انداخته...
و حال؟
حال... هیچ!
می توانی با اطمینان خاطر
نشانه ی قلب دیگری را
فتح کنی.

To the farm of my feelings

– My heart –

You will arrive

You will arrive!

You can review the map of my wounds

And learn:

Jumping without a parachute

Is joyful

And also painful.

Now that you have arrived at your destination

You run around

in the crowded alleys of my affection.

Suddenly

You will come across your fingerprints

imprinted...

On the walls of my heart

And Now?

Now...nothing!

Safely, you can master the directions

To another heart.

Mina Assadi

Date of Birth: 1943
Place of Birth: Sari
Place of Residence: Sweden
Education: BA, Journalism, University of Tehran
Profession: writer, journalist, playwright, and poet
Books: seven poetry collections

آب بالا آمد

آب بالا آمد
موج، اسبی شد
شیهه کشان
کف بر لب
و به سر منزل مقصود رسید

نشینیم که یأس
شوقمان را به برد
زندگی میل و تماشا دارد
چه کسی جرأت حاشا دارد؟

৽

Water Rose

Water rose
Wave turned into a horse
Neighing
Foaming at the mouth
And reached its ideal

Let's not sit and let despair
take away our joy
Life is filled with desires and spectacles
Who dares to deny that?

«ترانه ی خاوران»

در شعرهایم

من با تو از عشق

من با تو از شور

من با تو از امید گفتم

از تابش خورشید گفتم

اما نیامد از تو جوابی

همدرد خسته تا کی به خوابی؟

از تن فروش نه ساله گفتم

از مرگ تلخ آلاله گفتم

از خاوران خون و جنازه

از رویش صدها، هزاران لاله گفتم

اما نیامد از تو جوابی

همدرد خسته تاکی به خوابی؟

از کودکان گم کرده مادر

از مادران گم کرده فرزند

از مردمان بی جرم در بند

از مجرمان آزاد گفتم

از آرزوی بر باد گفتم

از دار و از اعدام و از بیداد گفتم

از چاله گفتم...از چاه گفتم

از نوجوان در راه گفتم

Song of Khavaran*

In my poems
I spoke to you of love
Of excitement
Of hope
I spoke of sunlight
Yet no response came from you
O weary friend, who shares my pain, how long will
    you stay asleep?
I spoke of the nine year old sex worker
I spoke of the bitter death of the Persian buttercup,
the Khavaran of blood and corpses
I spoke of the hundreds of thousands of tulips
    blooming
Yet no response came from you
O weary friend, who shares my pain, how long will
    you stay asleep?
Of children who lost their mothers
Of mothers who have lost their children
Of imprisoned innocents
I spoke of free felons
I spoke of hope blown away with the wind
I spoke of gallows, of execution, of injustice
I spoke of chasms...I spoke of abysses
I spoke of the adolescent in transit

---

* Khavaran is a district in southwest Tehran. Starting in the late
1980s, the cemetery there became infamous as the final resting
place of thousands of Iranians opposed to the regime, who were
murdered and buried there.

هرگز نیامد از تو جوابی

همدرد خسته تا کی به خوابی؟

࿐

بمباران

کودک

فرصت نیافت

که آخرین قطره ی چایش را بنوشد

فرصت نیافت

که کفش های کوچکش را به پا کند

فرصت نیافت

که کودکی های تابستانی اش را تکرار کند

و فرصت نیافت

که جوان شود.

به ناگاه

برقی در آسمان نیمه روشن سحرگاهی

صدایی بی مانند

و توقف زمان و زندگی

...

اینک

کفش کوچکی بر درگاه

فنجان معلق چای

کیف وارونه

دفترهای پاره ی مشق

گواه آنست

که دقایقی پیش از این سکوت مرگبار

Yet a response never came from you
O weary friend, who shares my pain, how long will
  you stay asleep?

❧

Bombardment

The kid
Didn't get the chance
To drink his last drop of tea
Didn't get the chance
To wear his tiny shoes
Didn't get the chance
To repeat his summertime child play
Didn't get the chance
To become a youth.
Suddenly
A spark in the half-lit dawn sky
An incomparable sound
And time and life stopped
…
Now
There's a tiny shoe in the doorway
The suspended cup of tea
Inverted bag
Torn notebooks
Are the testament
That minutes before this deadly silence

شوق زندگی و عشق
آفتاب این ویرانه بوده است

֎

در صدفی خواندم
و دریا
پر از آواز مروارید شد

֎

The excitement for life and love
Was the sunshine of this rubble

                    ❧

I sang in a sea shell
and the sea
filled with the song of pearls

                    ❧

Shabnam Azar

Date of Birth: 1977
Place of Birth: Shahi
Place of Residence: England
Education: MA Media Art, Academy of Media Art, Cologne,
  Germany
Profession: journalist, poet, multimedia artist
Books: four poetry collections

دست‌های خونی‌شان را
در جیب پنهان می‌کردند
شریک جرم بودند
اصرار داشتند بگویند
از روی ترس
روی از صحنه‌ی جرم
برگردانده بودیم
لبخندهای طبیعی می زدند
در حالی که ما می‌دیدیم
چگونه
چشم‌های‌شان

They hid their bloody hands
in their pockets
They were accomplices
They insisted that
fearful
we had turned away
form the crime scene
They smiled naturally
But we could see
that
their eyes

از قیرِ دروغ
سیاه شده بود
و چگونه
صورتشان
در مذاب تاریکی
فرو می رفت

෫

تو مثل من حرف نمی زنی؛ پس با تو نیستم
تو مثل من سکوت نمی کنی؛ پس با تو نیستم
تو مثل من نمی جنگی؛ پس با تو نیستم
تو مثل من کتاب نمی خوانی؛ پس با تو نیستم
تو مثل من شعار نمی دهی؛ پس با تو نیستم
تو سبز نیستی؛ پس با تو نیستم
بنفش نیستی؛ پس با تو نیستم
تو پرچمی داری که نمی شناسم
تو شاید حتی پرچمی نداری؛ پس با تو نیستم
تو خونی از تنت می رود
که به اندازه کافی سرخ نیست
من با تو نیستم

had turned black
with the tar of deceit
And their faces
were immersed
in the molten darkness.

❧

You don't speak like I do, therefore I am not with you
You aren't silent like I am, therefore I am not with you
You don't fight like I do, therefore I am not with you
You don't read like I do, therefore I am not with you
You don't chant slogans like I do, therefore I am not
    with you
You are not green* therefore I am not with you
You are not violet† therefore I am not with you
You carry a banner I don't recognize
Maybe you have no banner at all, therefore I am not
    with you
You bleed
A blood that is not red enough
I am not with you

---

* Green: The color of supporters of Ebrahim Raisi, a conservative
Iranian cleric who ran for president in 2017 but did not succeed
(he became president in 2021).

† Violet: The color of the supporters of Hassan Rouhani, a centrist
and reformist who served as the seventh president of Iran from
2013-2021.

تو می توانی بجنگی
من با تو نیستم
می توانی مجروح شوی
من با تو نیستم

تو حتی می توانی بمیری
در همین کوچه ها
من با تو نیستم
نه نمی توانی
برو گوشه ها
گوشه های کوچه ها
حتی برو دورتر دورترها
من با تو نیستم
مبادا خون تو کفش مرا کثیف کند!

You can fight
I am not with you
You can get wounded
I am not with you

You can even die
On these streets
I am not with you
No, you can't
Go to the corners
Corners of alleys
Go further than far
I am not with you
May your blood never stain my shoes!

Nahid Bagheri Goldschmeid

Date of Birth: 1957
Place of Birth: Tehran
Place of Residence: Austria
Education: [—]
Profession: author, translator, poet
Books: five poetry collections

بادبادك

شهروند سرگردانی ام
بادبادكی رشته گسیخته
گاه در فرود
پاكوب خشم باد
گاه در فراز
تا كاخ آفتاب

چیزی به شب نمانده است
كودك روزگار!
در كوچه های كدامین محله می گردی
بازیگوش؟!

Kite

I am a citizen of the state of wandering
A kite with a broken string
Sometimes descending
Dancing to the angry wind
Sometimes ascending
To the castle of the sun

Not much time left till nightfall
O child of Fortune!
In which alleys of which neighborhoods
Are you wandering
With your playful antics?

کی مهار خواهی کرد
این رشته به دست خویش؟
بر فراز کدامین خانه
خواهی افراشت
دل خوشی های خردم را
پرچم گون؟
سراغ داری بامی؟

❧

توفان

توفان که وزید
شاخه ها شکستند
درختان از نفس افتادند
و داس تیز باد،
آشیان پرندگان را درو کرد.
آرامش که دمید،
من ماندم و ویرانی
با هذیانی
از واژه های بی سر و دست
آرامش که دمید،
شادی از زمین کوچ کرده بود.

❧

When will you take
control of the string?
On which rooftop
will you raise
my small joys
like a flag?
Do you have a rooftop in mind?*

꩜

Storm

When the storm blew
The branches broke
Trees were out of breath
And wind's sharp sickle
cut the birds' nests.

When tranquility blew in
I remained and devastation
In a delirium
Of headless, armless words

When tranquility blew in
Joy had migrated from earth.

꩜

_____

*This poem has also been translated by Herbert Kuhner

باید بند کفش هایم را
محکم تر ببندم

راه می افتم
در بدرقه ی نگاه زنان
ترس خورده و پنهان
از پس دریچه های بسته

پیش می روم
در سایه سار کبود دیوارها،
و گام می کوبم،
بر سنگلاخ راهی ناهموار

هنوز منزل ها
تا مقصد باقی ست
شاید
از فصول باید گذشت
و یا از سالیان

همگام نیمروزی پریده رنگ
قد راست می کنم
و سینه را سپربلایی
که همواره در راه است

صورتم را که هنوز
از سیلی های شبانه سرخ است،
به بادهای شرقی می سپارم
و زیر ضربه های پیاپی اش

I must tie my shoe laces
More tightly

I start walking
Following the direction of the women's gaze
Fearful and hidden
Behind closed doors

I go further
In the azure shadow of the walls,
And I stomp my feet,
On an uneven stone path

There is still
A long way to the destination
We may have to
Traverse seasons
Or years

In unison with a pale noon
I stand tall
I use my chest as a shield
Against the disaster that is
Still on the way

My face, still red
from the nightly slaps
I entrust to the Eastern winds
And under its continuous lashes,

به خود می گویم،
هراسی نیست
باید به پیش رفت

بند کفش هایم را محکم بسته ام

I tell myself
Do not fear
Must go forward

I have tied my shoe laces tight*

---

* The poem, written to honor March 8, International Women's
Day, was sent to me by the poet.

Razieh Bahrami Khoshnood

Date of Birth: 1978
Place of Birth: Qom
Place of Residence: Iran
Education: Education: MA in Dramatic Literature
Profession: poet and translator
Books: four poetry collections

امروز جهان تعطیل است
تو اما فکر می کنی
این یک پنجشنبه معمولی است
و تمام مردم دنیا با تو هم عقیده اند!
حق با شماست
اتفاق مهمی نیفتاده است
من برای تو دلتنگم
همین

꧁

Today the world is closed
But you think
It's an ordinary Thursday
And everyone in the world agrees with you!
You are right
Nothing important has happened
I miss you
That's all.

این بزرگراه
تا انتهای جهان دور برگردان ندارد
و تمام خروجی هایش
به دوراهی چشم های تو میرسد
که بمانم و دوستت بدارم
یا برگردم و دوستت بدارم...

❧

دست های من
از روزی که رهایشان کردی
به موزه ی اشیای گم شده پیوست !

❧

همیشه راه حلی هست...
همیشه راه فراری...
پناه می برم از روزهای سختی که دوستت داشتم
به روزهای سخت تری که
دوستت خواهم داشت...

❧

This highway
Has no U-turn till the end of the earth
And all its exits
Arrive at the junction of your eyes
To stay and love you
Or come back and love you…

❧

My hands
Since the day you left them
Have become a part of the museum of lost things

❧

There's always a solution
There's always an escape route
I seek refuge from the difficult days when I loved you
in the more difficult days
When I'll keep loving you

❧

هی آقای پلیس!
که در شعرهای کودکی‌ام
مرد مهربانی بودی
تا مرا به آغوش مادرم برسانی
دلم گرفته بود که از خانه بیرون آمدم
و نمی‌دانستم
طبق تبصره‌های تازه‌ی قانون
وقتی که دلم می‌گیرد
باید کدام روسری‌ام را بپوشم

۶

گریه نکن
جهان پر شده از نمره‌های بیست
دانش‌آموزان زرنگتر
بمب‌های بزرگتری خواهندساخت
اگر قلب‌های کوچکتری داشته باشند
و هیچ کس
نمره مهربانی دست‌های تو را
وقتی به گربه‌های گرسنه غذا می دهی
در کارنامه‌ات نخواهد نوشت
دامن چین دارت را بپوش و بچرخ
جهان به ساز تو می رقصد
من برای معلمت نامه‌ای خواهم نوشت
و به او خواهم گفت
از مشق‌های زیاد که انگشت‌های کوچکت را خسته می کند
بیزارم

۶

Hey policeman!
In my childhood poems
You were a kind man
Who returned me to my mother's arms
Depressed, I had left the house
and I didn't know
Under the latest amendments to the law
When I am depressed
Which headscarf should I wear

❧

Don't cry
The world has become full of perfect scores
More intelligent students
Will make larger bombs
Even if they have smaller hearts
And nobody
Will give you a grade in your report card
for your kind hands that
feed hungry cats.

Wear your pleated skirt and twirl
The world will dance to the beat of your drum
I will write a note to your teacher
to tell her
that I despise
the copious homework that tires your small fingers.

❧

بگذار کودکم را شیر بدهم
نگران برگشت چک‌های تو باشم
شب‌ها که دیر به خانه می‌آیی
بهانه‌هایت را باور کنم
و تو را ببخشم.
بگذار زن باشم
من هابیلم را نمی‌کشم
یوسفم را در چاه نمی‌اندازم
هاجرم را در بیابان رها نمی‌کنم
و اسماعیلم را به سلاخ خانه نمی‌برم.
بگذار زن باشم
و تاریخ را تو رقم بزن

از روزها ی رفته ام
دری رو به آسمان می سازم
از روزهای نیامده ام
کوچه ای رو به آفتاب
و شعرهایم را
مثل نقلهای کوچك رنگی
در جیب کوله پشتیت می ریزم
●

بلند شو
تا بندهای کفشهای کو چکت را ببندم

Let me nurse my child
Worry about your bounced checks
The nights you come home late
I buy your excuses
And forgive you.
Let me be a woman
I won't kill my Abel
I won't throw my Joseph in a well
I won't abandon my Hagar in the desert
I won't take my Ishmael to the slaughterhouse
Let me be a woman
And you make history.

❧

From my bygone days
I build a door facing the sky
From my days yet to come
An alley facing the sun
And my poems
Like small colorful candies
I pour in the pocket of your backpack
•

Stand up
So I can tie the laces on your tiny shoes

❧

بهار و زمستان
روز و شب
دوستان و دشمنانم
همه می آیند و می روند
تنها و تنها مرگ است
که می آید و
می ماند

Spring and winter
Day and night
My friends and enemies
They all come and go
It's death and only death
That comes and
stays.

Roja Chamankar

Date of Birth: 1981
Place of Birth: Borazjan
Place of Residence: United States
Education: MA, Dramatic Literature, Tehran University, MA
  Cinematography, University of Strasbourg
Profession: poet, author, translator
Books: ten poetry collections

ما کنار دریا زندگی می کنیم
توی خشکی غرق می شویم
و آب
اولین درس از کتاب فارسی اول دبستان است
گوارای وجود
مایعی شفاف که می توان در آن
ماه فرسوده رادید
و خاك بر سر شده را چشید

ما در عطر نفت زندگی می کنیم
و آتش می گیریم
در گردباد می پیچیم

We live by the sea
We drown on dry land
And water
Is the first lesson in first grade Persian textbooks
Cheers!
A clear liquid in which
one can see the weary moon
And taste the earth covering our head

We live in the scent of petroleum and
We catch on fire
We twist in the tornado

و آسمان
خاکی تر از زمین
در حلقمان رسوب می کند
ما زیر بارشی سنگین
از عناصر سازنده ی دنیا
در حصاری از عدم
ما در مرکز خبر
در کنجی از جهان زندگی می کنیم

۶

از من
و روسری سفید و
دامنی لبریز از میخک
رفته بودی
برایم کمی جنوب بیاوری
و موی سیاهم را دوباره ببافی
حالا
بیست سال دیگر هم که بگذرد
چشمان تو
در چای هر شبم جا مانده

۶

And the sky
More dusty than the earth
Settles in our throats
We live under a heavy precipitation
of creative elements of the world
under the siege of absence
In the epicenter of news
In a corner of the world.

❧

You had left me
With a white scarf and
With a skirt brimming with carnations
To bring me back some southern charm and
To braid my black hair again
Now
Even after twenty years
Your eyes
Are left behind in my nightly tea

❧

جاده

از ستون فقرات گیسهایم می گذشت

لا به لای مو هایم توقف کردی

جاده از رگ ها

از دنده ها

جاده از مهره های پشتم می گذشت

نام شهرها ی بین راه را

لا به لای پوستم حك كردی

در من سفر نامه ای است

میراث مسیر های عا شقانه ات

۶

همیشه دری باز به در به دری بودم

رفتن را بیشتر از آمدن دوست داشتم

صدای تو تنها سرزمین واقعی ام بود

کلمات را در آغوشت پنهان می کنم

از این به بعد

همه می توانند شعر هایی از مرا

در تو بخوانند

The road
passing by the vertebral column of my tresses
You stopped in the midst of my hair
The road passing by my veins
My ribs
The road passing by my vertebras
You etched the name of the cities on the way
In the folds of my skin

Within me a travelog
The legacy of your romantic trajectories

I was always an open door to wandering
I preferred departures to arrivals
Your voice
Was my only true homeland
I hide the words in your embrace
From now on
Everyone can read my poems
Within you

Sareh Dastaran

Date of Birth: 1981
Place of Birth: Tehran
Place of Residence: Iran
Education: BA French Translation
Profession: journalist and poet
Books: one poetry collection

قهوه را شیرین می‌کنم
طعم لحظه‌ها فرقی نمی‌کند

❧

توفان

قطب‌نماها دیوانه شده‌اند
در سرگردانی من
و کسی نمی‌گوید
بادبان‌ها را بکشید
خشکی می‌بینم
خشکی

I sweeten the coffee
The taste of the moments doesn't change.

Storm

Compasses
Have gone mad
In my wandering
And no one says
Pull the sails
I see land
land

در من
توفانی است
که آرام نمی‌گیرد

۞

شب

پیش از خواب می‌چرخم
به سمتش
حرفی نمی‌زنیم
به هم نگاه می‌کنیم
من و
دیوار رو به رو

۞

آجرها و پرنده‌ها

عشق تو
پرنده‌ای بود
که جای یکی از آجرهای دیوار
لانه کرد

دیواری است
عشق تو
تک تک آجرهایش
پرنده

۞

Within me
There is a storm
That does not calm down

Night

Before falling asleep I turn
towards him
We do not speak
We look at each other
I and
the wall facing me!

Bricks and Birds

Your love
Was a bird
Nested in the place
of one of the bricks in the wall

Your love
Is a wall
Each of its bricks
A bird

فرصت از دست رفت

فرصت زیر یك سقف ماندن
از دست رفت
یا چتر باز نشد
یا باران بند آمد

❧

چه فرق می کند؟

چه فرق می کند
دوست داشتن یا دوست نداشتن

هر دو
پیراهن یوسف را دریدند

❧

ماه

شك ندارم
ماه را
دلتنگی من
کامل کرده است

Lost Opportunity

The opportunity to to stay under the same roof
Was lost
Either the umbrella did not open
Or the rain stopped

What Difference Does It Make?

What difference does it make
To love or not to love?

They both ripped open
Joseph's shirt

The Moon

I have no doubt
That it is my longing
Which has
Made it a full moon

Sadaf Derakhshan

Date of Birth: 1974

Place of Birth: Shahriar

Place of Residence: Iran

Education: PhD, Persian Language and
  Literature; BS Chemical Engineering

Profession: author, instructor, researcher, and poet

Books: two poetry collections

تمام لحظه های با تو بودن ام را
قاب گرفته ام
به در و دیوار زده ام
دیوارها هم
خشت به خشت
تو را لمس می کنند

Each and every moment I have been with you
I have framed
I have hung on every wall
The walls too
Brick by brick
Feel you

به
موازات من نیا
که تا ابد مرا به تو نمی رساند
مقابل دست هایم بنشین
تا نقطه تلاقی ما
چشم های تو باشد

❧

چشم هایت
میان سطر سطر
شعرهایم چه می کنند؟
نه می توانم بگویم ببند
نه می توانم بگویم ببین

Don't walk parallel to me
for you will never reach me
Sit in front of my hands
So that your eyes
Will be our meeting point

What are your eyes doing
In the midst of
the lines of my poems?
I cannot ask that you close them
I cannot ask that you see!

Maryam Eshaghi

Date of Birth: 1969
Place of Birth: Gilan
Place of Residence: Iran
Education: MD
Profession: pediatrician, writer, and poet
Books: four poetry collections

وطنم
آغوش توست
از مرز تو، آن سوتر
به زبان غریبه ای حرف می زنند

❧

دوست داشتن ات
جاده ای بی انتهاست
و من
راننده ای مست
که خدا برایش دست تکان می دهد

❧

My Homeland
is your embrace
Beyond the borders of your body
They speak a foreign language.

❧

Loving you
Is an endless road
And I
A drunk driver
to whom God is waving

❧

یادم باشد
یکی از روزهای همین اردیبهشت
شعر کوتاهی بنویسم
با کلماتی از یخ
از دی ماه بلندی که در من است

‹›

روزی
موهایم را از ماسه تکاندم
صدایت را بوسیدم و گذاشتم کنار
و کلید همه‌ی واژه‌ها را قورت دادم

‹›

I should remember
One day this April
to write a short poem
with words of ice
Of the long January within me

One day
I shook the sand out of my hair
Kissed your voice and set it aside
And swallowed the key to all the words.

Leila Farjami

Date of Birth: 1972
Place of Birth: Tehran
Place of Residence: United States
Education: MA Psychology
Profession: psychotherapist, poet
Books: 7 poetry collections

خواهرم

خواهرم زنی ست خندان
ایستاده رو به دوربین
پشت سرش
برج ها و خانه ی های مسطح مابین
آنتن ها و ماهواره ها و کبوترهای دود گرفته
سرخسهای خانگی بیجان

My Sister

My sister is a smiling woman
Standing in front of a camera

Behind her
Flat houses and towers
Between antennas and satellites
Smoke covered pigeons
And lifeless ferns

خواهرم زنی ست خندان
گاه روی کوچه ای حوالی امیر آباد تیر می خورد و دراز می کشد
می آیند و می برند و در بهشت زهرا دفنش می کنند
گاه زیر پلها می ایستد
لبهایش را سیاه می کند و نرخ روز را اعلام
سوار ماشینی می شود که معمولاً راننده اش زشت است
و می رود دور دورها.

گاه روی مبل به گریه می افتد

شاید به خاطر شوهری که نداشته ست

یا بچه ای که نخواهد داشت

خواهرم زنی ست خندان
و همه ی تهران مال اوست
سراغش را می توانی از هرکس و هر جایی بگیری
و بپرسی آخرین بار چه خورده است
چه گفته ست
چه شنیده ست
و در کدام خرابه خوابیده ست
و چرا
هروقت تا بلند می شود
دوباره
به زمین می افتد؟

My sister is a smiling woman
Sometimes she gets shot on alleys around Amir Abad*

And she lies down

They come and take her

And bury her in Behesht-e Zahra†

Sometimes she stands under bridges
Paints her lips black and announces her rate for the day
She gets in a car and drives far away with an ugly thug,
Sometimes she is reduced to tears on the sofa
Maybe because of the husband she hasn't had
Or the child she won't have.

My sister is a smiling woman
And all of Tehran belongs to her
You can ask anyone, anywhere about her
And ask what she last ate
What she said
What she heard
In which ruin has she slept
And why
Every time she tries to get up
She falls down again?

᳘

---

*A neighborhood in Tehran, Amir Abad is known for its alleys and long streets.

† The largest cemetery in Iran, Behesht-e-Zahra is on the outskirts of Tehran.

چهار اپیزود از مرگ

۱
خواب می دیدم که راه می رفتم
(راه تو بوده ای)
به سنگی خوردم
مرگ بود
باز گشتم
مرگی دیگر

(مرگ تو بوده ای)
آن دو
(آن دو!)
زندگی
جای دیگری
نبود.

۲
موهایش را بلند می کند
گُلی می کارد در انتهای هر تار
ابرها پلکهایش را می سایند
باران می گیرد
و بر خاک می ریزد
فکر می کند زنده است
نامش را گذاشتند مرگ
و من خواندمش:
گِل.

Four Episodes of Death

1

I was dreaming of walking
(you were the road)
I ran into a rock
It was death
I returned.
Another death

(You were death)
Those two
(Those two!)

Life
Was
in no other place.

2

She grows her hair long
Plants a flower at the end of each strand
Clouds rub against her eyelids
It starts to rain
And it pours on the ground
(She) thinks she is alive
They called it death
And I called it
Mud.

۳

زیباترینها هم می میرند
مرگ همان قورباغه ای ست که به بوسه ات
شاهزاده ای می شود
و تو را به قصر بلورینش باز می گرداند،
جایی که پس از سالها در اعماق چاه
و شنیدن صدای قلوه سنگ هایی بر آب
فراموش کرده بودی.

۴

مرگی در پس

مرگی به پیش

زندگی

میان پرده ای

از صحنه هایی صامت.

3
The most beautiful die too
Death is the frog who turns into a prince with your
　kiss
And returns you to his glass castle

A place you had forgotten about
After many years in the depth of the well
And hearing the sound of pebbles on water

4
A death behind you
A death in front of you

Life:
An intermission
of silent scenes

Niki Firoozkoohi

Date of Birth: [—]
Place of Birth: [—]
Place of Residence: Norway
Education: [—]
Profession: author, poet
Books: six poetry collections

سه روز است که یکبند باریده
انگار گنجشک‌ها مرده اند
به جای آوازِ پرنده
در گوشِ من
اسبی شیهه می‌کشد
من از شهوتِ یک بعداز ظهر خالی شده ام
اینجا
این اتاق
این تخت
این خانه
هوسِ بودن را از من گرفته است
سه روز است که باریده
من و چشم‌های بی انگیزه ی من

It has been raining incessantly for three days
I think the sparrows have died
Instead of a bird's song
A horse neighs
In my ear
I have become emptied of a lustful afternoon
Here
This room
This bed
This house
Have taken away my will to live
It has been raining for three days

پر می‌شویم
از خیال
رویا
انتظار
حدس
حدس یک صدا
صدا ی پای کسی که می‌آید
که حدس می‌زنم می‌آید
خش خش یک چتر
انتظارِ یک دست
یک آغوش
کسی که در یک بعد از ظهر دل گرفته
بعد از سه روز که یکبند باریده
هوس بودن با من را دارد
شاید ... شاید ... شاید ... گنجشک‌ها هنوز نمرده باشند.
سه چیز را برای هیچکس آرزو نمیکنم ... تنهایی ... سه روزِ
بارانی ...
و این دو سوال، میایی؟؟ نمیایی؟؟

؏

با من مدارا کن
در سینه ی من
مرغکی باران خورده
سراسیمه
دل می‌زند
بالش را بگیری

My aimless eyes and I
Are filled
With dream
Hope
Anticipation
Guess
A guess as to a sound
The sound of the footsteps of someone approaching
That I guess is coming
The rustling of an umbrella
The anticipation of a hand
Of an embrace
Someone, who on a gloomy afternoon
After three days of incessant rain
Desires to see me
Maybe…maybe…maybe
The sparrows have not yet died
I do not wish three things on anybody…
    Loneliness…Three rainy days…
And these two questions: Are you coming? not
    coming?

Put up with me
In my chest
A rain-soaked little bird
Frightened
Beats
If you hold its wing

چنان صاعقه خورده ای
یکباره
تهی می‌شود
رهایش کنی
از آخرین شاخه ی بودن
بی صدا
فرو می‌پاشد
با من مدارا کن
تا بهار
تا رسیدن
تا دریای شمال
تا خاک‌های مرطوبِ شهرمان
چیزی نمانده
با من مدارا کن
بگذار دلهره ی جدایی را
در حافظه ی هیچ عاشقی شکوفا نکنیم
با من مدارا کن
بگذار دلهره ی جدایی را
در حافظه ی هیچ عاشقی شکوفا نکنیم

❦

مردهای زیادی
با خیالِ من خوابیده اند
با چشم بسته
مرا سر تا به ناخن
عریان دیده اند
گیسوانِ سیاهم را ناز کرده اند
نازم کشیده اند

Like one struck by lightening
It empties all at once
If you set it free
From the last branch of being
Silently
It falls apart
Put up with me
Until spring
Until arrival
Until the northern sea
the soaked soil of our city
We are almost there
Put up with me
Let's not allow separation anxiety bloom
In the memory of any lover

❧

Many men
Have slept thinking of me
With eyes shut
They have seen me naked
From head to toe
They have caressed my black hair
They have caressed me

خواب دیده اند
خواب دیده اند
شب‌های زیادی به دنیا پشت کرده ام
سیگار کشیده ام
کنارِ بغض‌هایم درد کشیده ام
برایِ آغوشی که نیست آه کشیده ام
یکی از این شب‌ها تو می‌آیی
خواب دیده ام
خواب دیده ام

They have dreamt
They have dreamt
Many nights, I have turned my back to the world
I have smoked
I have endured pain alongside the lump in my
    throat
I have sighed for the embrace that does not exist
One of these nights, you will come
I have dreamt
I have dreamt

Leili Galehdaran

Date of Birth: 1976

Place of Birth: Bushehr

Place of Residence: Italy

Education: PhD, Digital Technology in Theatre, Sapienza
   University of Rome

Profession: university professor, poet

Books: three poetry collections

نانِ روزانه ی منی
گاه سیرم می کنی با زندگی
گاه سیرم می کنی از زندگی.

نانِ روزانه ی منی
تا فرو روی
زخم می اندازی گلوگاه ساکت مرا
با این همه اما
جز تو
گرسنه نمی شوم

You are my daily bread
Sometimes you fill me with life
Sometimes you make me fed up with life.

You are my daily bread
As you go down
You scratch my silent throat
With all this, however
Except for you
I don't get hungry

روی نگاهم
غلیظ
و
داغ
چه قهوه‌ای می‌ریزد
چشم‌هایت
عرق می‌کند
نگاهم
و مست می‌کنی.

❧

دلم برایت تنگ می‌شود
حتا وقتی روبه‌رویم نشسته‌ای
و نگاه تو دور می‌شود از مماس نگاهم
تا فنجان چای
قول بده
قول بده
تنها دست‌های من زیر سیگاری‌ات باشد.

❧

والزّیتون

طوفان شروع می شود
جفت مرا نوح فراموش کرده است
کاش کفتری که می پرانی
هیچوقت شاخه زیتون نیاورد

❧

On my gaze
Thick
And
hot
What a coffee that pours out
Your eyes
Sweat
My gaze
You become drunk

❧

I miss you
Even when you are sitting across from me
And your gaze becomes distant from the brush of
    my gaze
To the cup of tea
Promise
Promise
That only my hands be your ashtray

❧

By the Olive*

The storm hits
Noah has forgotten my pair
Hopefully the dove you release
Will never bring back an olive branch

❧

---

* The Fig surah in the Qur'an begins by mentioning the fig and
the olive.

کرئون

کرئون
با دستها مکبث در دست
ریچارد سومی همدست
بر صحنه های تکرا رشدنی
آنتاگنیست های تکراری
و آنتیگنه ای مکرر در ما
با مشتی خاك از دست رفته
که بر سر کنیم یا
بر برادران ممنوع التدفین مان بپاشیم؟

Creon

Creon
With Macbeth's hands in his hands
Accomplice Richard III
In a recurring scene
Repetitive antagonists
Antigones recurring within us
With a fistful of lost soil
To bury us
Or to scatter on our brothers
Whose burials are prohibited?

Ghodsi Ghazinour

Date of Birth: 1946
Place of Birth: Langarood
Place of Residence: Netherlands
Education: BA Fine Arts (Painting), Tehran University
Profession: artist (painter), author, poet, children's literature
Books: six poetry collections

کاش آدم هم مثل شتر
کوهان داشت
تا شب های مهتابی
کوهانش را پر از ستاره می کرد
برای شب های گرفته ی ابری.

୨

کاش هنوز هم به همدیگر
دروغ های کودکانه می گفتیم
این حقیقت عریان بی حیا
به چه درد می خورد

୨

I wish humans had a hump
Like that of a camel
So on moonlit nights
They could store the stars
For their gray overcast nights

❧

I wish we were still telling each other
childish fibs
What is the use of
this audacious naked truth?

❧

قصه های بلند
پُرند از لحظه های پوچ
تو قصه ی کوتاهی.

۞

بعد از آن همه سرگردانی،
تو قصه ی کوتاهی
روی وجب به وجب خاک
بعد از آن همه جستجو روی نقشه های جهان،
دانستم دستان توست وطن من!

۞

آدم برفیم من
تو آفتاب.
در نگاه
آب می شوم، آب.

۞

بند به پایم زدند که بمانم
گسستم و رفتم
تو بال دادیم برای تنهایی
رها گشتم و ماندم!

۞

Long tales
are filled with hollow moments
You
are a short story

༄

After wandering all over
every inch of the earth
You are a short story
After searching all over
the world atlas
I learned that your hands are my homeland!

༄

I'm a snowman
You, sunlight.
In the gaze
I melt, melt.

༄

They shackled me so I would stay
I broke away and escaped
You gave me wings for my loneliness
I was liberated and I stayed

Sholeh Golrokhi

Date of Birth: 1973
Place of Birth: Birjand
Place of Residence: France
Education: Diploma (Natural Sciences)
Profession: poet
Books: one poetry collection (not yet published)

این جا پاریس است
من توی زیباترین خیابان پاریس هستم
پشت پنجره ای که بسیار کوچك است
و تو از همه ی این خانه می گذری

خانه او رو به روی خانه ی ماست
که روزی پیدای اش کردم
یك روز که آفتاب روی پرده افتاده بود
و من به آن دست کشیدم
آن وقت خانه او روبه روی خانه ی ما بود
با چند شمع روشن
وکسانی که از اتاق هایش رد می شدند

Here is Paris
I am on the most beautiful street in Paris
At a tiny window
And you pass by this entire house

The house is facing ours
and I found it one day
A day when sunlight was shining on the curtains
And I ran my hand over it
At the time, there was a house facing our house
With some lit candles
And people who would pass through its rooms

من اتاق سوم را دوست داشتم
چون شمع های بیشتری داشت

من می دانم
آن جا زنی زندگی می کند
که عاشق بوی قهوه است
و هر روز گل های تازه می خرد
آن جا مردی زندگی می کند
که زن را دوست دارد
و هر شب ماه را نشانش می دهد
آن ها می دانند کسی از پنجره نگاه شان می کند
چون هرروز زیباتر از روز قبلشان می شوند
زن که از کنار پرده می گذرد
و مردکه همیشه در آغوش اش می کشد

آن ها می دانند
کسی نگاه شان می کند
اما اشك های مرا نمی بینند
و پرنده ی کوچکی را
که هراسان به پنجره می خورد
و پایین می افتد...

ﹸ

پرنده هایی دارم
که در پیراهنم زندگی می کنند
وقتی دعوایم می کنی
مهربان می شوند
وقتی مهربانی
دعوایشان می شود

ﹸ

I liked the third room
Because it had more candles

I know
A woman lives there
Who loves the smell of coffee
and buys fresh flowers everyday
A man lives there
Who loves the woman
And every night shows her the moon
They know that someone watches them through
    the window
Because each day they are more beautiful than the
    last
The woman who passes by the curtain
And the man who embraces her

They know
Someone is watching them
But they don't see my tears
nor the little bird
Who, frightened, crashes into the window
And falls down

❧

I have birds
Who live in my dress
When you fight with me
They become kind
When you are kind
They fight

❧

روزهاست
که تو رفته ای
من مانده ام بدون پا
برای به دنیا آمدن

❧

از روزهایی برایم بگو
که این شهر را باد می‌بَرَد
من با دخترم روی آب
صبحانه می‌خوریم
من غرق می‌شوم
دخترم قایق

❧

من خواب دیدم یك مرد
آمد میان باغ
سیب ها را نگاه کرد
سیب ها پر از لب های او شدند
باران گرفت
خواب من سرخ شد
و آسمان به سرخی نشست
به ماه نشست
خانم نشست روی ماه
با لب های سرخش
و سیب ها از دست هایش
سر خوردند توی حوض
من خواب دیدم

Many days have passed
since you left
I remain without legs
for being born

❧

Tell me of the days
When the city is blown away by the wind
My daughter and I on the water
Having breakfast
I drown
My daughter, becomes a boat

❧

I dreamt that a man
Came to the orchard
Looked at the apples
Apples filled with his lips
It started to rain
My dream turned red
The sky turned red
It spread to the moon
The lady sat on the moon
With her red lips
And the apples in her hands
Slipped into the small pool
I dreamt of

حوض را پر از پرنده های نارنجی
که هی می افتادند
و تو هی می افتادی توی حوض
خانم روسری اش را کشید
دلش را به بام داد
وپرید

A small pool filled with orange birds
Who'd repeatedly fall
And you'd repeatedly fall into the small pool
The lady adjusted her scarf
entrusted her heart to the roof
and jumped

Elham Gordi

Date of Birth: 1981-82
Place of Birth: Tehran
Place of Residence: United States
Education: BS Laboratory Sciences & Social Work
Profession: translator, researcher, and poet
Books: Two Poetry Collections

دست نجار است
که صندلی را تکان می دهد
وگرنه درخت ها
از مهاجرت خوششان نمی آمد
خوششان نمی آمد
به آنها بگویی «میز
صندلی کمد»

❧

It's the carpenter's hand
that moves the chair
Otherwise trees
wouldn't like emigration
Wouldn't like
to be called "table,
chair, cupboard"

❧

کرسی
پر از خاطرات یلدا بود
شبی که در انباری
به حبس ابد
محکوم میشد

※

The Korsi[*]

Was full of memories of Yalda[†]

The night it would be sentenced to life

In the storage room

* Similar to the Japanese *kotatsu* or Spanish *brasero*, a *korsi* is a low table covered with a heavy blanket or quilted comforter and with a heat source under it. Charcoal is traditionally used as the heat source, though nowadays the table may also be electrically heated. During the winter months, families gather around the *korsi* to chat and get warm, and to celebrate special occasions.

† The winter solstice, *Yalda* in Persian, is the longest night of the year. Iranians celebrate on this night by gathering with their loved ones, eating dried fruits, nuts, pomegranates and watermelon (kept over from the summer for this purpose). The pagan origin of this tradition was to support the sun/light/good to conquer and overcome darkness/evil to rise again on the next day. Traditionally they also recite Persian poetry, especially those written by the acclaimed Iranian poet, Hafez.

Taraneh Habib

Date of Birth: 1954

Place of Birth: Mashhad

Place of Residence: United States

Education: MA English Literature, George Mason
  University; BA English Language and Literature,
  Ferdowsi University

Profession: poet, writer

Books: One collection of poetry

باد
با پروازی بلند چرخید
و در دورها گم شد.
پرنده دنبال بالهایش گشت.
نبود
انگار که
باد آنها را ربوده بود!

The wind
Flying high, circled
Got lost somewhere in the far distance
The bird anxiously searched for its wings
Nowhere to be found
As if
The wind had stolen them!

حوا در بهشت
دنبال سیب می گشت
و نمی دانست
که شیطان
آن را
در گلوی آدم
پنهان کرده است.

❧

فریادهای فرو خورده
در گلویم
تبدیل به آه می شوند و
چون نسیم
در بهار می وزند.

❧

نگاهش
به تلخی نگاه آن پرنده بود
که تیر خورده
صیاد را می نگریست.

❧

نور
مأیوسانه
دنبال ستاره ای می گشت
که میلیون ها سال پیش

مرده بود.

❧

In Paradise, Eve
was looking for the apple
And she didn't know
the devil
has hidden it
in Adam's throat.

❧

Silenced screams
In my throat
Turn into sighs and
Like the breeze
Blow in springtime.

❧

Her look
Was as resentful as
the wounded bird
glaring at the hunter.

❧

The light
Was hopelessly
Searching for a star
That had died a
million years ago.

Roya Hakakian

Date of Birth: 1966
Place of Birth: Tehran
Place of Residence: United States
Education: BA Psychology, Brooklyn College
Profession: journalist, writer and poet
Books: one poetry collection

از گریستن ها - بخش ۱

لکه ی درشت
بر مخمل سفید برف
گوهری رنگین
بر گردن سیاه شب
باد می وزد
و من
در ساحل گرم خانه
پهلو می گیرم.

Of Sobs—Part 1

A large stain
on the white, velvet snow
A colorful gem
around the neck of the dark night
Wind blows
and I
Dock on
the warm shores of home.

ده ساله بودم
آنروز که گرفتار صاعقه شدم
هیولایی توپ و عروسک را از من ستاند —
و من برهنه و گریان
یکباره بزرگ شدم
و تشویش‌هایی عظیم
شیطنت‌های بچگی را خاکستر کرد
جادوگری سیاه‌پوش خنده را بر لبهایم جادو کرد —
دیگر هرگز از تاریکی نترسیدم
چراغ اشرف دشمنان شد
روشنایی بود که راه بر اژدها مینمایاند
تاریکی مادر من بود
و پدر...
هیچ نبود.
دیوی یک‌شاخ —
با کمربندی از آتش
کودکی‌ام را از من ربود.
من آنروز ده ساله بودم.

I was ten years old
The day I was caught by lightning
A monster took away my ball and doll –
And I, naked and tearful,
Grew up at once
And severe anxieties
Turned childhood antics to ash
The spell of a witch in a black cloak put a smile on
    my lips –
I no longer feared the dark
Light became the noblest of adversaries
It was light that had showed the way to dragons
Darkness was my mother
And father…
was not there.
A one-horned demon –
With a belt of fire
Robbed me of my childhood.
I was ten years old then.

Farideh Hassanzadeh

Date of Birth: 1952
Place of Birth: Tehran
Place of Residence: Iran
Education: BS, English Literature, Library Science
Profession: translator, poet
Books: one poetry collection

از کنار یکدیگر می‌گذریم
من به سوی آشپزخانه
تو به سوی دفتر کار
سهم من کوه ظرف‌ها و رخت‌های نشسته
سهم تو انبوه پرونده‌های زاینده.
از کنار یکدیگر می‌گذریم
گاه بی‌نیم‌نگاهی به یکدیگر
تنها به نیمه‌شب‌ها شاید
تن‌های ما فرصتی یابند
برای سخن گفتن با یکدیگر.

We pass by each other*
I am headed to the kitchen
You are headed to the office
My share: the mountain of dishes and unwashed
    clothes
Your share: the heap of multiplying files
We pass by each other
Sometimes without a brief glance at one another.
Maybe only at midnight
our bodies find the opportunity
to speak to each other.

---

*Another version of this poem was previously translated by
Sheema Kalbassi.

با این همه شک ندارم

به رغمِ سکوتِ فرساینده

به رغمِ ملالِ آزارنده

زمین فقط به خاطر تو تکرار می‌کند شب را و روز را

و لحظه‌ای که نباشی

قلب خورشید از کار می‌افتد

❧

نه دریا دریا نامه‌های عاشقانه‌ات

در صندوقچه مخملی خاطرات

نه پاکت پاکت باغ‌های پرمیوه و بهشتِ آغوشت

در غروب‌های به خانه بازگشتن:

و نه حتی هدیه هجده عیار جشن سالروز ازدواج‌مان

در جمع شاهدان عینی

تنها گواه قلب صادق و عاشق تو

همین سطلِ پلاستیکی‌ِ قرمزِ فرسوده، سنگین از زباله هرروزه

که هر شب، هر چقدر هم خسته باشی

پله پله، چهار طبقه تمام پایین می‌بری،

بی‌نیم نگاهی حتی

به تعارفِ تکراریِ دستانِ خواب‌آلوده‌ام!

❧

With all this, I have no doubt

Despite the tiresome silence

Despite the bothersome pain

It is only for you that the earth repeats the days
    and the nights

And the instant you are gone

The heart of the sun will stop

❧

Neither sea upon sea of your love letters

In the velvet chest of memories

Nor paper bags upon paper bags of fruit filled
    orchards

Nor the safe haven of your embrace on evenings
when you return home:

And not even the eighteen carat gold gift for our
    wedding anniversary

Offered before eyewitnesses

The only testament of you pure loving heart

The worn out red bin, heavy with everyday trash

That no matter how tired, everynight

you take it, step by step, down four flights

Without even a glance

At the repeated offer of my sleepy hands

❧

بس نیست ؟

از خیرِ عشق گذشتم
و به آرامشِ سایه‌ها و خاطره‌ها
قناعت کردم

زمان از گذشتن درماند
و دقیقه‌ها و لحظه‌ها
زیرِ بارانِ بمب‌ها منفجر شدند

شب که می‌شود
دیگر رؤیاهایم را مسواک نمی‌زنم.
شب که می‌شود
دیگر برای خورشیدِ گم شده در آسمان دل نمی‌سوزانم

شب که می‌شود
ماهِ ترسیده را در آسمان رها می‌کنم
و به زیرِ زمین پناه می‌برم

دیگر نه زنم، نه شاعر

شب به شب
واقعی‌تر می‌شوم
مثلِ آتشبارهای ضدهوایی
مثلِ آژیرهای زرد و قرمز و آبی
مثلِ بمب‌هایی
که خاکستر و ویرانه را
به واقعیت بدل می‌کنند
شب به شب واقعی‌تر می‌شوم
و شب به شب پیرتر
آن قدر پیر که در آینه

Isn't It Enough?

I gave up on love
And settled for
The tranquility of shadows and memories.

Time failed to go on
While minutes and seconds
Exploded under the carpet bombings.

When night arrives
I no longer brush my dreams
When night arrives
I no longer pity the lost sun in the sky

When night arrives
Leaving alone the scared moon in the sky
I take refuge in the basement.

I am no longer a woman, nor a poet.

Night after night
I become more real
Like the flaming anti-aircraft missiles
Like the yellow, red and white alarms
Like the bombs
That turned destruction and ashes into reality
Night after night I become more real
Night after night I grow older,
So old that in the mirror

دیگر هیچ نمی بینم
جز یك ردیف صندلی خالی

بس نیست ؟
بس نیست؟

انسان جز یك تکه نان
یك شب خوابِ راحت
و یك بغل بی پناهی
مگر چه می‌خواهد؟

ॐ

خاطرات یک مرده

از دنیای فانی
منظرهٔ گلدان‌های شمعدانی را دوست داشتم
پشتِ پنجرهٔ خانه‌ها
و بوسهٔ باد را بر حجابِ اجباری
در جست و جوی گیسوانم
هلاكِ راه رفتن بودم زیرِقطره های باران
و لبریز شدن از امیدِ یافتنِ نیمهٔ گمشده
بیزار بودم از پوسترهای نامزدهای انتخاباتی
و قاب‌های عکسی که در ادارات و بانک ها
عینِ میخ فرو می‌رفتند در چشم‌هایم
زیرا زمان را ردِ پای شاهان و رؤسای جمهور می‌دیدند
سیر نمی‌شدم از تماشای مشت‌های گره کرده
امواجی که از انتهای دریاها برمی‌آمدند گهگاه
برای شستنِ همهٔ ردِ پاها الا آزادی، صلح و عشق
برای رنگین کردنِ خونِ زندگی در رگ‌های مرگ

ॐ

I see nothing
But a row of empty chairs

Isn't it enough?
Isn't it enough?

Other than a piece of bread
A good night's sleep
And an armful of unreachable dreams
What does a human need?

❧

Memories of a Dead Woman *(Posthumous Poem)*

Of the fleeting world
I liked the sight of geranium pots
behind the house windows
And the wind's kiss on compulsory hijab
In search of my tresses.
I was dying to walk under the raindrops
overflowing with hope of finding my lost half.
I hated the campaign posters for political candidates
And the framed pictures in offices and banks
Poking me in the eye like a nail
For, they saw time as the footprints of kings and presidents.
I never tired of seeing clenched fists
Waves coming from the end of the sea, every now and then
To wash away the footprints of all but freedom, peace and love
To color the life blood in the vessels of death.

Hengameh Hoveyda

Date of Birth: 1978

Place of Birth: Tehran

Place of Residence: France

Education: PhD Sociology and Political Philosophy,
  Sorbonne

Profession: writer, researcher, and poet

Books: 3 poetry collections

اینجا روشن تر از آن است
که چشمهایت چیزی را ببینند...
کدام آنها خودشان اند؟
از خودت می پرسی
اما خود شان هم
نمی دانند ...
هیچکدام!
اسامی مستعار واقعی ترند
آنها
نقابشان خودشان است.

It's too bright here

for your eyes to see anything…

Which of them are themselves?

You ask yourself

But they themselves don't even know…

None of them!

Aliases are more real

Their masks are who they are

اسامی واقعی مدعی اند
حقیقت دارند
و دروغشان در حقیقتشان است.

ॐ

و آن اندك روشنایی در دوردست
وهمی که سو سو می زند
در کلمات
و سکوتی
که از ما نیست
خدایی است گریخته از المپ
همچون نیزه ای فرو رفته
در لبهایمان

Real names claim

to be true

And their artifice is in their truth

꙰

A dim light in the distance
A delusion that flickers
In words
And a silence
That is not ours
There is a God who fled from Olympus
Like an arrow deeply lodged
In our lips

Maryam Jafari Azarmani

Date of Birth: 1977
Place of Birth: Tehran
Place of Residence: [—]
Education: PhD, Persian Literature, Alzahra
  University; BA, French
Profession: literary critic, translator, poet
Books: seventeen poetry collections

مداد قرمزم می‌گفت از کشتار بنویسم
— نه مثل بچه‌ها روی در و دیوار بنویسم —

مکرّر بود تصویری که دنیا روبه‌رویم کاشت
ولی از من توقّع داشت بی‌تکرار بنویسم

خدای شعر، زندان‌بانِ من بوده‌ست از اوّل
که حبسم کرده در این خانه تا بسیار بنویسم

چه توهینی از این بدتر که در دنیای بی‌معنی
برای زنده بودن شعرِ معنی‌دار بنویسم

My red pencil told me to write of massacres
rather than doodle on walls like a little kid

The world planted before me a repeating image
Yet it expected me to write unique works

From the beginning, the God of poetry has been
  my warden
Imprisoned me at home to write copiously

In this meaningless world what worse insult is there
than writing meaningful poetry in order to live

با پنجره‌ای خسته، پس حال تماشا نیست
پس خوب نمی‌بینم پس منظره زیبا نیست

می‌بندم اگر زشت است، زشت است که می‌بندم
دنیای پر از در هم، بی‌پنجره دنیا نیست

انسانم و ممکن نیست آزاد بیَندیشم
وقتی همه‌ی فکرم در جمجمه زندانی‌ست

شعر است که می‌بیند آن نقطه‌ی پایان را
نقطه سرخط، شاعر بنویس که من، ما نیست

ﹻ

یادت شراب و خنده فراهم می‌آوَرَد
یک مریمِ جدید برایم می‌آورد

دیروزهای من به شکایت گذشت، حیف
غُر می‌زدم که شعر فقط غم می‌آورد

حالا ولی شنیدنِ هر عاشقانه‌ای
یادِ تو را «به خاطرِ مریم» می‌آورد

هر ابر عینِ توست در اشکالِ مختلف
در چشم‌هَام چشمه‌ی زمزم می‌آورد

Through a tired window, there is no desire to look
So I don't see well, the view is not all that pretty

I'll shut it if it's ugly, it is ugly therefore I shut it
A chaotic world; no window, no world

I am human, impossible to think freely
when my thoughts are imprisoned in my skull

Poetry can see the endgame,
Period.
New paragraph.
Write, O poet!

That I, is not we!

༄

Thoughts of you bring wine and laughter
They reveal a new Maryam!

My yesterdays, filled with complaints, alas!
I grumbled that poetry brings but sorrow

Today all love songs
Bring you to Maryam's thoughts

Every cloud, differently shaped, resembles you
It brings the fountain of Zamzam* to my eyes

---

*It is a spring near Ka'abe, Mecca, Saudi Arabia. Pilgrims believe Zamzam's water to be holy.

خط جنسِ سیم نیست، نسیم شنیدن است
تا می‌وزد صدای تو را هم می‌آورد

هی گریه می‌کنم که طبیعت فقط تویی
شعرم در این زمینه چرا کم می‌آورد؟

☙

آنقدر سنّتی‌ام
که با دوربینِ همین گوشی
می‌توانم عکسِ واقعیِ سعدی را
با کاغذ گلاسه
بردارم وُ روی کلّیّات بچسبانم
تا هر روز ببینم
که روی قفسهٔ بالای کتاب‌خانه نشسته است.
اگر ببینی باور نمی‌کنی چقدر با نقاشی‌اش فرق دارد

آنقدر سنّتی‌ام
که نورش توی چشمم می‌زند
وقتی درِ یخچال را باز می‌کنم
چه شب‌ها که از صداهای عجیبش
از خواب پریده‌ام
و فکر کرده‌ام که شاید
روحی، جسمی، چیزی میزی در آشپزخانه تکان می‌خورَد

آنقدر سنّتی‌ام
که هرچیزی را
همانطور که دوست دارم می‌بینم
اجاق گاز را یک مشت هیزم لعاب‌زده

The line is not of wire, it's the breeze of sound
As it blows it also carries your voice

I constantly cry that nature is only you
Why does my poem fall short in this context?

❧

I am so traditional that
I can take a true picture of Sa'adi
with my cell phone camera
Print it on coated paper
Paste it on his collection of poems,
So that I can see him on the top of the bookshelf
everyday.
Seeing it, you won't believe how different it is from
    a painting of him

I am so traditional that
when I open the fridge door
the light inside bothers my eyes.
Many nights I am awakened by its strange noise
and have thought that
a ghost, a body, something is roaming
in the kitchen.

I am so traditional that
I see things
the way I like to see them
I see the stove

شیر آب را حفره‌ای عمیق بین سنگ‌ها که به قول بچه‌ها

کاشی‌های دیوارند

و حتا همین دوربینِ گوشی

چشمِ برزخیِ من است

باور نمی‌کنی چه چیزهایی می‌بینم

❧

هستم که می‌نویسم بودن به جز زبان نیست

هرکس نمی‌نویسد انگار در جهان نیست

من آمدم به دنیا، دنیا به من نیامد

من در میان اویم، اویی در این میان نیست

آتش زدم به بودن تا گُر بگیرم از تن

حرفی‌ست مانده در من، می‌سوزد و دهان نیست

لکنت گرفته شاید، پس من چگونه باید

بنویسمش به کاغذ، شعری که در زبان نیست

❧

as coated firewood
The faucet
as a deep hole between rocks
like tiles on a wall
as the kids would say.
And even this cell phone camera
is my damned eye
You can't believe the things I see.

꙰

I write therefore I am, language is being
Whoever does not write, is not living

I came to the world, the world didn't become me
I am in the midst of it, yet there is no it

I set existence on fire, my body aflame
Something's left in me to say, it burns but there's no mouth

Maybe it's the stuttering, but how shall I
put on paper what's not on the tongue

꙰

اگر به جای «خوابِ یک ستارهٔ قرمز»

فروغ را می‌دیدم

از خواب می‌آوردمش بیرون

با همان روسریِ دههٔ چهل

که جنسش دیگر پیدا نمی‌شود

خیابان‌ها را نشانش می‌دادم

– طبق معمول کسی ما را نمی‌شناخت –

می‌بردمش میدانِ ولی عصر،

تا «زنانِ سادهٔ کامل» را ببیند

که با لباس‌های مُبدّل‌شان از اداره بر‌می‌گردند وُ

هرگز نمی‌توانند «روی لیوان‌ها» برقصند

وَ مردان را

که با دامن سفید

در آشپزخانه‌های شهر، رقص مدرن آموخته‌اند

آنقدر دور می‌زدیم تا

در مترو دلش بگیرد وُ

ترافیک خسته‌اش کند وُ

اصلاً از رانندگی بدش بیاید وُ هشتاد ساله شود وُ

وقتی اسمش را سرچ می‌کنم

پس از خواندنِ تمام حرف‌های مجازی، بگوید:

If instead of the "dream of a red star"*
I'd dream of Forough
I'd take her out of my dream
With her same sixties scarf
Which material can no longer be found
I'd show her the streets
 – As usual, no one would recognize us –
I would take her to Vali Asr circle,
to observe "simple complete women"
returning from work in their costumes
And could never dance "on the water glasses"
And men
wearing white skirts
who, in kitchens around the city, learned modern
    dance

We'd go around until
She gets claustrophobic in the metro and
the traffic makes her tired and
She gets totally fed up with driving and
She turns eighty and
When I search her name
After all virtual talks, she would say:

———————

* The words in quotation marks are lines of three of Forough
Farrokhzad's most famous poems. Forough Farrokhzad (1934-
1967) is a Persian poet who broke many social norms with her
poetry. She openly wrote about subjects that were considered
taboo, including sexual desire. "Dream of the red star," "eyelid"
and "shoes pair up" are lines in the poem "The One Who Is Like
Nobody Else"; "Simple complete women," and "dance on water
glasses" are lines in the poem "The Green Illusion."

مریم! چرا «پلک چشمم» نمی‌پرد و «کفش‌هایم جفت» نمی‌شوند

༃

پنجِ صبح است، حتماً تو خوابی، طبق معمول بیدارم این‌جا

از سرِ شب نخوابیده‌ام هیچ، چون به یادت گرفتارم این‌جا

دوست دارم که تنها تو باشی، با من و این غزل‌های وحشی

بی‌خبر بی‌خدا بی‌تعلّق، هِه! چقدر آرزو دارم این‌جا

می‌شود در تخیّل فرو رفت، تا سر از جای دیگر درآورد

رقص و آزادی و... بی‌خیالش! از سیاست چه بیزارم این‌جا

خواب دیدم کنارم نشستی، روی بازوی تو گریه کردم

هرچه گفتم تو باور نکردی: بی‌تو من سر به دیوارم این‌جا

بچه باش و کمی خط‌خطی کن! بر تنم پوستم شعر بنویس

کاملش گفتنی نیست، بگذار تا سه تا نقطه بگذارم این‌جا

❦

Maryam! Why isn't my "eyelid" twitching
And why won't my "shoes pair up"?

༒

Five AM , you are surely asleep, I am, as usual
  awake over here
Haven't slept a wink all night, cos I am consumed
  by thoughts of you here

I wanted only you, with me and these wild gazelles
No news, no God, no belonging! I have so many
  hopes here

It's possible to daydream and end in a different
  place
Dancing and freedom...forget it! How I hate the
  politics here

Dreamt of you next to me, cried on your shoulder
Didn't believe a word I said, without you I am
  sorrowful here

Be a child and doodle! Write poetry on my body,
  my skin
The complete version is unspeakable, let me end
  with an ellipsis here...

Nahid Kabiri

Date of Birth: 1948
Place of Birth: Kermanshah
Place of Residence: United States
Education: BA Social Sciences, University of Tehran
Profession: writer, poet
Books: Twelve Poetry collections

آرزوها ی پاییزی

در آخرین روزها ی پاییز
به آخرین شعله ی برگها نگاه می کنم
که به سرخی خون ها
به زردی بی وفایی ها
و نارنجی رویا ها
بر زمین می غلتند
به جاده های خالی طولانی

Autumn Wishes

On the last days of Fall
I look at the last flames of the leaves
Red like blood
Yellow like unfaithfulness
Orange like dreams
Tumbling to the ground
On long deserted roads

انتظارهای عبث
و آرزوهایی که
دانه دانه
با برگ ها
فرو می ریزند

ᕲ

زنان تابستان

در روزهای مخملی زرد
زنان سبز تابستان
زیر چتر های قرمز خورشید
نشسته اند و
با خارش بنفش دست هاشان
از تفاله های ترش
آبغوره می گیرند
خربزه ای در حوض
شر شر آبی در پاشویه
شاخه های ترد و خالی تاک
آسمانی نمناک
و من کوچک کوچک آن جا

Futile expectations
and dreams
Fall
One by one
With the leaves.

Summertime Women

In the yellow velvety days
Green women of summer
sitting
Under the red umbrella of the sun
With the purple scratching of their hands
Extracting verjuice
from the sour pulp.
A yellow melon floating in the small pool
Water splashing in the foot basin
The bare fragile vines
A drizzling sky
And I, small, small,

در گهواره ای
که جیر جیر چوبی پایه هاش
اعصاب ام را
از همان روزها
خرد می کند
...

بی لالایی خوابیده اند ستاره ها
کلمه ها روی شب راه می روند
باد فاصله های سکوت را
می شکند
سایه ها دلتنگی هاشان را
به پاییز می آورند
نشانی نیلوفر
مرداب است.
تو نگران تاریکی اما نباش
ماه
در شمال آویشن ها
به دنیا خواهد آمد.

there
In a cradle
with creaking wooden legs
That ever since those days
get on my nerves.

Stars have slept without a lullaby
Words are walking on top of the night.
Wind breaks silent distances
Shadows bring their sorrow
to the Fall
The address of the waterlily
is the swamp.
But you should not worry about the dark
The moon
will be born
north of the thyme fields.

Samaneh Kahrobaeian

Date of Birth: 1979
Place of Birth: Mashhad
Place of Residence: Tehran
Education: MA in Sociology, University of Tehran; BS in
  Mechanical Engineering, Ferdowsi University
Profession: Design Engineer, poet
Books: Two collections of poetry

رفیق

خوشا رفیق که پیشش نقاب برداری
عیان کنی که چه اندیشه‌ها به سر داری

خوشا رفیق که در خانه‌اش خراب شوی
شبی که هیچ نداری و چشم تر داری

Friend

Blessed to have a friend before whom you remove
    your mask
To whom you can reveal the thoughts on your mind

Blessed to have a friend whose home you can crash
On a night you have nothing but tears in your eyes

که بی‌دریغ قبولت کند چه خوب و چه بد
اگر فضاحت و ننگ و اگر هنر داری

تو را عجیب نداند، بفهمدت تا کُنه
گمان کنی که ز خود نسخه‌ای دگر داری

خیال پشت خیال تو پر دهد تا صبح
اگر نیاز به تکثیر بال و پر داری

دلت نلرزد و سودا کنی، نپرهیزی
چنین که ضامن خوشنام و معتبر داری

رفیق و پشت و پناه و محافظ و کس و کار
تبار و طایفه و مادر و پدر داری

به اکتشاف جهان می‌روی سفر خوش باد
که همسفر چو خودت طالب خطر داری

۲

به بازجوی درون فرصت سوال مده
خیال سفسطه دارد، به او مجال مده

Who accepts you unconditionally, rotten or
    righteous,
Whether you are disgraced, dishonored or virtuous

Who does not find you strange, understands you to
    the core
So you trust you have another copy of yourself

Who will give wings to your dreams until a new
    dawn rings
If what you need is wind beneath your wings

You will not fear, you'll wheel and deal, you will
    not forbear
for you have a reputable and esteemed sponsor

A pal, a pillar, a protector, a posse
You have a clan, a tribe, a mother and a father

About to discover the world, happy trails!
With a companion, who like you, seeks danger!

ஒ

Don't give the internal investigator the chance to
    inquire
He intends to use deceit, don't let him

بدان مفتش ناپاک، جان پاک نبخش
بدان حرامی دون، بوسه‌ی حلال مده

همین تکیده و تنها که می‌روی خوب است
گزیده باش دلا! تن به ابتذال مده

شکستگی مرضی مهلک است، محکم باش
نگاه دار غمت را و انتقال مده

در انتظار پذیرش نباش، بیهوده است
به این توقع مسموم پرّ و بال مده

به آفرین و ملامت کم و زیاد نشو
عنان صبر به فریاد قیل و قال مده

به احتمال طلوعی دوباره فکر نکن
یقین بدان که چنین است، احتمال مده!

۸

اهلی شدۀ ستم کشیده
افسردۀ در قفس چپیده

کت بستۀ کند گشته دندان
بی یال و دمِ زبان بریده

Don't give the filthy inspector your pure soul
Don't give a pure kiss to the tainted wretch

Going along, as you are, gaunt and solitary, is just
    fine
Wait to be chosen, my heart! Don't settle for
    ordinary!

To be broken is a deadly disease, be strong!
Keep your sorrow to yourself, don't pass it on!

Don't wait for acceptance, it's useless!
Don't let this toxic delusion take flight

Don't let praise or reproach determine your worth
Don't place the reins of patience in the hands of
    discord!

Don't question the possibility of a new dawn
Trust that it will happen, don't question it!

❧

Domesticated oppressed
Caged depressed

teeth dulled, hands tied
No mane, no tail, tongue-tied

فرسودهٔ سرد و گرم دنیا
خشک و تر روزگار دیده

صد دفتر یاوه را به اکراه
از بانگ بلندگو شنیده

خالی شده از امید و باور
در بستر مرگ آرمیده

با مردم زنده هم قبیله
با مردم مرده هم‌عقیده

با آنهمه شرم و بردباری
چون تیغ به استخوان رسیده

از جور زمان فغان برآرد
تیغ از بن استخوان برآرد

۞

ذهنت، زبانت، راه و رفتارت دوگانه
هر حرکتت وارونه هر کارت دوگانه

چیزی فراتر از ریا، سنگین‌تر از زرق
قلبت دورو، قانون و معیارت دوگانه

پوشیده در شال و قبا، عریانِ عریان
جسمت سلامت، جان بیمارت دوگانه

Worn out by life's hot and cold
Having seen life's ups and downs

Having reluctantly heard a hundred nonsensical books
from a roaring loudspeaker

Devoid of all hope and belief
Lying in a deathbed

Of the tribe of the living
Like-minded with the dead

With all that shame and patience
The blade has cut to the bone

From the wailing of life's grief
The blade has lifted from the depths of the bone

❧

Your mind, your tongue, your manners: duplicitous
Each movement contrary, each action: duplicitous

Beyond hypocrisy, heavier than deceit
Your heart two-faced, your rules and values: duplicitous

Cloaked in a long robe, completely naked
Your body healthy, your sick soul: duplicitous

گرگ حریص خلوت و خرگوش جلوت
نقش طلبکار و بدهکارت دوگانه

همرنگ مردم زیستن، مجبور و شاکی
بیچاره! ای میمونِ اطوارت دوگانه

گفتن، غلط کردن، نوشتن، حذف کردن
دفترچهٔ مخدوش اشعارت دوگانه

𝒸

نخست شور جوانی کبوتر از من ساخت
گلو برید و سپس بالش پر از من ساخت

چو مادیان خرامان دشت‌ها بودم
که بار بردن بسیار استر از من ساخت

بسیط زبر زمین فلس بر تنم رویاند
غریب جانوری شوم و منکر از من ساخت

زمان مجسمه سازی لجوج و ماهر بود
به ضربه‌های قلم غول مرمر از من ساخت

نمی‌شناسم و خود را غریبه می‌یابم
تراش تیشه‌ی غم شخص دیگر از من ساخت

جهان یگانگی‌ام را به ابتذال کشید
هزار نسخه‌ی با هم برابر از من ساخت

A greedy wolf in private, a sheep in company
Your role as creditor and debtor: duplicitous

Conforming, obliged and dissatisfied
Poor thing! Your simian antics: duplicitous

Speaking, making mistakes, writing, deleting
Your crossed out collection of poems: duplicitous

❧

First, the excitement of youth turned me into a dove
Cut my throat, made the feather pillow I now embody

Like a mare, I strutted in the fields
Carrying heavy loads, a mule I now embody

The rough and vast terrain grew scales on my body
A strange and sinister creature I now embody

Time was a skilled and stubborn sculptor
With strikes of its pen, a marble giant I now embody

No recognition, I am a stranger in my own body
With strikes of the ax of sorrow, a different person I
    now embody

The world rendered my uniqueness moot
One of a thousand copies I now embody

مذاب کرد مرا وانگهی به قالب ریخت
نمونه‌های زمخت و یُقُرتر از من ساخت

هنوز هسته‌ی داغم مذاب و سوزان است
سمانه بودم و آتش سمندر از من ساخت

؏

کجا برده است قایق را تقلّاهای پارویی
به جای شاه‌ماهی صید کردم بچه میگویی

پری‌هایی که پنهانند در موجی کف‌آلوده
مرا بردند سوی او، به افسونی، به جادویی

تلف کردم فسونم را، ندارد هیچ معنایی
برایش پیچش مویی، اشارتهای ابرویی

بریدم، پاره کردم، لت زدم، از ته تراشیدم
مگر زنجیر را عبرت شود تعذیب گیسویی

شبیه ماهی‌ام، انداخته در تابه‌ی داغی
که شب تا صبح می‌غلتم ز پهلویی به پهلویی

به یغما برده‌ای امنیت ما را، عجب کاری!
به هیچ انگاشتی شخصیت ما را، عجب رویی!

It melted me then poured me into a mold
A sturdier, coarser version I now embody

My burning essence is still molten and torrid
I was a Samaneh* but in the fire a salamander I now
   embody

꙳

Where has all the oar's struggle taken the boat?
Instead of a sturgeon I caught a baby shrimp

Mermaids hidden in spumous waves
Took me closer to him, magically, spellbound

I wasted my spell, it's all meaningless to him
My curls, my beckoning brow

I cut, I tore, I slapped, I shaved it all off
May the sentencing of the hair be a lesson for the chain

Like a fish, thrown in a hot frying pan
I toss and turn restlessly all night long

You have robbed us of safety, well done!
You took us for nothing, what audacity!

---

*Samaneh is the poet's first name. It means quail.

سلامم می‌دهی اما در آغوشم نمی‌گیری
برای مستحبّی واجبی را ترک می‌گویی

۵

خیری از خوبی ندیدم شور شر برداشتم
خیش و خرمن را رها کردم تبر برداشتم

سر به زیر افکنده بودم در مناجاتی عبث
نامجاب و بی‌جواب از سجده سر برداشتم

این چه رنجی بود، جایی تنگ و جانی در عذاب
چشم امّید ار حیات مختصر برداشتم

سنگِ بالا برده از کوهم فروغلتید و رفت
هرچه گندم کاشتم زقّوم تر برداشتم

زآن حریر پاره پاره، زآن لباس قلوه کن
زآن تن عریان بی‌حرمت نظر برداشتم

You greet me but won't hold me in your arms
You leave the required* to pursue the recommended*

❧

I saw no benefit in being good, I committed to being bad
I put down the plow, the harvest, and took up the ax

I had bowed, in the midst of a useless prayer
Prayer unanswered, with no reply, I no longer bow

A cramped space, a tormented soul: what horrid
   suffering!
I lost my hope in this brief life

The boulder I pushed uphill rolled back and dropped
Though I planted wheat, I sowed Zaqqoum†

I turned away from the shredded silk organza
The torn dress, this disgraced naked body

---

* Religious notions as to what is prescribed and what is not
prescribed, but merely suggested

† According to the Qur'an, Zaqqoum or Zaqqum (Arabic: زقوم) is a
tree that "springs out of the bottom of Hell." It is mentioned in verses
17:60 (as the "cursed tree"),[1] 37:62-68,[2] 44:43,[3] and 56:52,[4]
of the Qur'an.

تا کجا جنگیدن و تسلیم، پرواز و سقوط
دست از این تکرار پوچ بی‌ثمر برداشتم

تا بدین حد کُند و سنگین، سرب و آهن، سست و لَخت
عاقبت برخاستم بار سفر برداشتم

ﻉ

﷾

خوبم ولی نه مثل جوانی‌ها
با خنده‌ها و مزه پرانی‌ها

زل می‌زنم به مردم و می‌خندم
شاید کمی شبیه روانی‌ها

این سال‌های تلخ پر از آشوب
این اضطراب‌ها، نگرانی‌ها

این سال‌ها خطوط بدی انداخت
بر چهره‌ام نشاند نشانی‌ها

اخمی شبیه صورت سلّاخان
زخمی چنان قیافه‌ی جانی‌ها!

چون موریانه ذهن مرا خورد
فکر دسیسه‌ها و تبانی‌ها

Fight, surrender, flight, crash to what end?
I gave up on this futile inane cycle

Painfully slow and heavy, lead and iron, loose and
    smooth
Finally I rose and packed to leave

❧

I am fine but not as fine as my youth
With all the laughter, all the banter

I stare at people and laugh
A little like the deranged

These bitter, turbulent years
these anxieties, these worries

These years caused deep wrinkles
 They left their mark on my face

A scowl like the expression of slaughterers
A wound like the expression of murderers

Like a termite has eaten away my brain
thoughts of conspiracies and collusions

دوران ما به خاطره پیوسته
چون باجه‌ها و پنج قرانی‌ها

ما مانده‌ایم و ترکش جامانده
از انفجار ما عصبانی‌ها

❧

برای دیدن روی تو استخاره گرفتم
چنان که خواسته بودم نشد، دوباره گرفتم

دلت گوزن جوان بود و فصل دام گذاری
من آن گوزن جوان را به یك اشاره گرفتم

میان برکه‌ی غمگین چشم‌های سیاهت
شبانه غوطه زدم چند تا ستاره گرفتم

مرا جنون زده دیدی و در کنار گرفتی
من از تمام جنون جهان کناره گرفتم

کنار مادر انگور مثل دایه نشستم
به مهربانی از او طفل شیر خواره گرفتم

دو هفته دختر رَز گریه کرد زار و فغان زد
براي خواب چهل روزه گاهواره گرفتم

Our era has become a memory
Like old fashioned kiosks, out of circulation coins

We only remain, with the shell casings
caused by the explosion of our anger

࿊

To see your face or not? I performed bibliomancy
I repeated it as it didn't strike my fancy

Your heart, a young stag and at hunting season
I captured that young stag with a single gesture

In the pond of your sorrowful black eyes
At night, I dove in and picked some stars

You took me as mad and held me by your side
I, in turn, withdrew from all the madness in the world

Like a wet nurse, I sat next to mother vine*
With utter kindness I took the nursing infant

Daughter of Raz,† teared up, groaned and moaned
   for two weeks
I got a crib for the forty day slumber

---

* Daughter of raz: grape (wine)

† Mother: the vine

شبی بنوش به شادی اگرچه تلخ نماید
من از خلاصه‌ی اندوه خود عصاره گرفتم

به شوق کعبه دویدم، خراب و خسته رسیدم
نشد طواف کنم، نایب الزیاره گرفتم

୬

چنین خوش است که آدم بدن نداشته باشد
به غیر روح در این پیرهن نداشته باشد

کمد شود شکمش تا غذا درآن بچپاند
رهد ز لذت خوردن، دهن نداشته باشد

کشو شود بطنش، بچه را در آن بگذارد
که شوق کاشتن و داشتن نداشته باشد

بتن بریزد و سیمان کند تمام زمین را
خدا نکرده گل و یاسمن نداشته باشد

Tonight, drink this bitter wine joyfully
For the wine is the extract of my sorrows*

I ran to Kaaba eagerly, arrived tired, worn out
Unable to complete the pilgrimage, appointed a
  surrogate†

❧

It is best that a human not have a body
That he have but the spirit under his clothes

That his stomach become a cupboard stuffed with
  food
That he not enjoy eating, not have a mouth

That his belly become a drawer, contain a child
That he not desire conceiving nor having a child

To pour concrete and cement all over the ground
God forbid roses and jasmines grow there

---

*The last six lines depict the process of wine making

† This poem uses the lexicon of *Khamrieh*, the literature of
drinking and drunkenness. The expression "Daughter of Raz"
depicting grape and/or wine was used by Rudaki, who lived
in the tenth century, and is known as the first poet writing in
Persian. Other poets who have written famous *Khamrieh*s include
Bashshar Marghazi (tenth century) and Manuchehri (eleventh
century).

به انحراف نیافتد خطوط صاف و ردیفش
که انحنا و کمان و شکن نداشته باشد

نوای ساز نپیچد، صدای خنده نیاید
به غیر نوحه بیت الحزن نداشته باشد

اگر جسارت بیجا کند کسی و برقصد
مجال نشرش را مطلقاً نداشته باشد

شود جمیع عوالم همه مذکر و سالم
خوشا به حال جهانی که زن نداشته باشد

ॐ

نگاه کن به درختان خشک در مهتاب
به شاخه های تکبده به آیه های عذاب

چراغ های روان در بزرگراه مهیب
چنان که برتن کوهی گدازه های مذاب

مرا به خانه ببر ساعتی نوازش کن
در ازدهام خیابان و شب مرا دریاب

بروج شوم فلك کرده اند جادویم
بیا رصد کن و پیدا کنم به اسطرلاب

That its smooth, orderly lines not deviate
That there be no curvature, no arch, no crease

No echo of an instrument's music, no sound of
    laughter
That it have nothing but mournful songs

If someone is brazen enough to dance
Broadcasting it must be prohibited

All possible worlds will be masculine and healthy
Blessed is a world with no woman in it

꙳

Behold the dry trees under the moonlight
The bare branches, the verses of agony

Light pouring in a scary highway
Like molten lava on the sides of a mountain

Take me home and caress me for a while
Rescue me from the crowded street, the night

The sinister constellations have cast a spell on me
Come, observe and find me with an astrolabe

کباب شد دل آن ماهی زلال پرست
به شب نشینی خرچنگ های این مرداب

چگونه می گذرد روزها ی بی تابی؟
نپرس آن چه نخواهی که بشنویش جواب

نپرس بی تو و بی عکس یادگاری تو
که بوی گل ز که جوییم در غیاب گلاب

دو مستطیل مزاحم، در مستطیل عبوس:
فضای خالی خانه، فضای خالی قاب

هزار جهد بکردم که سرّ عشق بپو...
که وزن شعر درست است و حال شعر خراب

۶

The heart of the fish who worships clarity
Was seared in this swamp's feast of the crabs[*]

How are the restless days going?
Don't ask if you don't want to hear the answer

Don't ask that without you, without your picture
From who should we seek the scent of the rose in
    the absence of rose water[†]

Two intruding rectangles, two grim rectangles
The empty space of the house, the empty space of
    the picture frame

I tried a thousand ways to hi….the mystery of love
The poem's rhyme is sound, its content in disrepair

꽃

)

---

[*] Refers to a poem by Mohammad-Ali Bahmani, a contemporary poet born in Dezful Iran in 1942. He has both classical and modern poems. This is line 3 of his poem "Swamp Crabs."

[†] Refers to a poem by Molana (Rumi) in *Masnavi-ye Ma'navi* *"The Spiritual Couplets,"* book 1, part 33, line 5.

Sheema Kalbasi

Date of Birth: 1972
Place of Birth: Tehran
Place of Residence: United States
Education: Nursing, Social Studies, History
Profession: literary translator, documentary filmmaker,
  human rights advocate, poet
Books: four poetry collections

بی‌نام

شب که می خوابم از شعر بیدار می شوم
می خواهم بنویسم. می گویم: نه
نه. دیگر شعر نمی نویسم. شعری که اسم تو در آن پر نباشد
پالتوی کارمندیست در اداره دارایی
که همیشه آویزان است
ارباب رجوع سراغ که می گیرد
پالتو را نشان می دهند: هست
و من می گویم: الان که زمستان نیست

Nameless

When I sleep at night I am awakened by poetry
I want to write, but I say: No!
No. I will no longer write poetry.
A poem without your name
is like a Ministry of Treasury employee's overcoat
permanently hung on the coat rack
When the customer asks for him
They point to the overcoat: He is here
And I say: but it's not winter

ژیواگو

زنی بودم با تنپوشی از گیپور
و برایت شعر می خواندم

امروز

وقت خواندن ندارم
و لایه ای از وازلین
به پاشنه های ترک خورده پاهایم نشسته.

بیا عشق بازی کنیم.

Zhivago

I was a woman with a robe of guipure
And I used to recite poetry for you

Today

I don't have time for reciting poetry
And a layer of Vaseline
Has settled on my cracked heels.

Let's make love.

Mohaddaseh Kalhor

Date of Birth: 1997
Place of Birth: Tehran
Place of Residence: Iran
Education: BA
Profession: painter, poet
Books: one poetry collection

کنارم مینشینی تو
نگاهت میکنم غرقم
مگر دیده کسی در عمر
که معبودش کنارش چای مینوشد؟؟؟

❧

باران نم نم
بوی خاك
ولیعصر شلوغ
و من تنها!
حتی دیگر آسمان هم با او دست به یکی کرده است...

❧

You sit next to me
Your gaze drowns me
Has anyone ever seen
Their idol drink tea next to them?

❧

Drizzle
Smell of earth
Crowded Vali Asr Avenue and
I, alone!
Even the sky has colluded with him now…

❧

Guity Khoshdel

Date of Birth: 1951
Place of Birth: Tehran
Place of Residence: Iran
Education: BA, English Literature, Tehran University
Profession: translator, poet
Books: eight poetry collections

کدام آهنگ را تصویر کنم؟
سال دوم دانشکده ادبیات را
غروب است و به بخاری تکیه داده ام،
پتوی چهارخانه سفید و سرمه ای روی زانوانم،
شکسپیر می خوانم،
فردا با خانم صورتگر کلاس دارم
موهایم را با بیگودی پیچیده ام
در قلبم هیجانی که نامش را نمی دانم حرکت می کند،
گویی با شکسپیر هماهنگم، هنوز معنای خویشتن را نمی‌دانم،
دختری بیست ساله ام: شاعر...
عاشق گنجشکهایی که درحیاط دانشکده پرواز می کنند

ﻊ

Which song shall I illustrate?
Sophomore year, studying literature
It's dusk, I'm leaning on a heater
The checkered navy and white blanket on my knees,
Reading Shakespeare,
Tomorrow I have a class with Ms. Souratgar
Curlers in my hair
An unfamiliar excitement moving in my heart
As if I am in lock step with Shakespeare
I still don't know the essence of my self
I am a twenty year old girl: a poet
In love with the sparrows flying around the
   University's yard

از مخروبه ای که به معبد می رسید گذشتم
گردن بندی از طلا که نام من بر آن حک شده بود
میان گل و لای افتاده بود. نمی دانستم آیا آن را بردارم؟
گفته بودی نامها را فراموش کنم، شکلها را...
سرانجام یك مشت نور در کف دستم بجا خواهد ماند

خودم را می فریبم که گمان می برم
از دل داستانی که خود نوشته ام، بر می خیزی
چگونه؟ هیچکس در عالم بیرون
ترا نیافریده است...
تو همان جرعه شرابی که هزار سال است
وعده اش را داده اند.
تو، یك تکه نانی که بوی شعر می دهد

I passed by the ruins leading to the temple
A gold necklace with my name engraved on it
Had fallen in the mud, I didn't know whether to
    take it
You had told me to forget the names, the shapes…
At the end, a fistful of light will remain in my hand.

I fool myself when I believe
you will rise from the heart of the story I've written
How? Nobody in the outside world
has created you...
You are the sip of wine
promised for a thousand years.
You, the piece of bread that smells of poetry.

Leila Kordbacheh

Date of Birth: 1981
Place of Birth: Tehran
Place of Residence: Tehran
Education: PhD in Persian Literature, University
  of Isfahan
Profession: researcher, literary critic, poet
Books: Eight collections of poetry

از میان تمام واژه‌های دنیا
تنها نام تو را دوست دارم؛
واژه‌ای که مرا به گریه می‌اندازد
واژه‌ای که مرا به خنده می‌اندازد
واژه‌ای که طرز ادای حروفش را دوست دارم
با چشم‌های خودت ببینی
تا خاطره‌ای بردارم از حیرت آشکارت

من
خاطرات زیادی از تو ندارم امّا
زیاد به تو فکر می‌کنم

Of all the words in the world
I only love your name;
The word that brings me to tears
The word that makes me laugh
The word whose enunciation I love
I wish you could witness it with your own eyes
So that I could capture the memory
of your obvious surprise

I
don't have many memories of you
But I think of you often

و از هر خیابانی که می‌گذرم،
قبلاً درحالِ فکر کردن به تو از آن گذشته‌ام

درحال فکر کردن به تو راه می‌روم، آواز می‌خوانم
درحال فکر کردن به تو می‌خوابم، بیدار می‌شوم
درحال فکر کردن به تو زندگی می‌کنم
درحال فکر کردن به تو
یک آن یادم می‌افتد که دیگر
چیز زیادی برای تجربه کردن نمانده است

چیزی
برای تجربه کردن نمانده است،
آنقدر با تو زیسته‌ام بی‌تو
که فکر می‌کنم دیگر
می‌توانم بمیرم

ᔖ

یک روز
می‌آیم انتهای همان کوچه،
مقابل آن ساختمان بلند می‌ایستم،
به خودم می‌گویم: «ببین
جایی‌که آخرین‌بار بوسیدمش
با خاک یکسان شده،
و از ویرانه‌اش خانه‌ای غریبه روییده
دیگر او از آهن و آجر که محکم‌تر نبود؟»

ᔖ

And as I pass through each street
I am reminded of previous times
when I was thinking of you as I passed through them

I think of you as I walk, as I sing
I think of you as I sleep, as I wake up
I think of you as I live.
As I think of you,
All of a sudden, I realize
That there's not much else left to experience

No other
experience is left
I have lived with you for so long
That I think
Finally I can die.

❧

One day
I will come to the end of that alley
I will stand in front of that tall building
And I will whisper: "Look, where I last kissed him
has been demolished,
And the rubble has given rise to a strange house
Surely, he could not be stronger than iron or brick?"

❧

با دویست‌وچند تکه استخوانم دوستت دارم
(و چندسال باید بگذرد؟)
(تا استخوان‌های آدم، همه‌چیز را فراموش کنند؟)
با من بگو
بگو قلب‌ها فراموشکارترند
یا استخوان‌ها؟

با من بگو
بگو مثل خواب، که گاهی از دست‌هایم شروع می‌شود، گاهی از
پاهایم
پوسیدن از قلبم آغاز می‌شود،
یا استخوان‌هایم؟

تو شبیه پرستوها هستی
وقتی با کوچ بی‌هنگامی بهار را به خانه‌ام می‌آوری
وقتی با کوچ بی‌هنگامی بهار را از خانه‌ام می‌بری

بخوان
با هر زبانی که عاشقانه تر است
آهنگین تر است
و واج‌های صمیمی‌تری دارد
بخوان

I love you, with all my two hundred and some
   bones
(and how many years will it take for human bones
   to forget things?)

Tell me
Tell me whether hearts are more forgetful
Or bones?

Tell me
Tell me like a numbness
that sometimes starts with my hands,
sometimes with my feet,
Does decay originate in my heart,
Or in my bones?

             ✧

You are like swallows
When with an untimely migration you bring
   spring to my home
When with an untimely migration you take spring
   away from my home

Recite!
In the most loving
musical language
with the most intimate phonemes
Recite!

حتی اگر شده اندازهٔ پنجرهای

که بیش از حوصلهٔ بهار بسته ماندهست

آنقدر بسته ماندهست

که اسمش را گذاشته اند دیوار.

❧

می خواهی دلتنگت نباشم

می خواهی

دلتنگت نباشم

انگار که بخواهی،

شیروانیهایِ «رشت» خیس نباشند.

انگار که بخواهی

زمستانهایِ «الموت» سرد

انگار که بخواهی

پاییزهای روستای چنار «کاشان» زرد.

دنیا اما کاری به خواستنِ هیچکس ندارد.

من هم سالهاست

می خواهم کنارم باشی

❧

Even the size of a single window
which has remained closed, trying spring's patience
closed for so long
that is now called a wall

❧

You Want that I Not Miss You

You want
That I not miss you.
It is like your wanting
that gable roofs in Rasht* not be wet
It is like your wanting
that Alamut winters not be cold
It is like your wanting
that the autumns in Chenar village of Kashan not be yellow.
The world, however, does not care about what anyone wants.
For many years, I, too, have wanted
that you be next to me

❧

---

*Rasht, near the Caspian Sea has a wet climate. Alamut, a mountain near
Qazvin, is very cold. Chenar, the name of the village in Kashan in northeast
Iran means "plane tree" the leaves of which turn yellow in the autumn.

به خاطرات بیشتری از تو نیاز دارم
تا بضاعت سال های پیری ام باشند
سال هایی که یك زن
به خاطرات عاشقانه بیش ازمستمری ماهانه نیازدارد،
به دکمه ی افتاده ای از پیراهنت مثلاً
به رد انگشتت بر شیشه ی عینکم مثلاً
به فندکی، تار مویی، چیزی مثلاً...

به چیزهایی که بعدها نگاهشان کنم
و باورم بشود که در روزهایی از عمرم
واقعاً زنده بوده ام
واقعاً
یك زن زنده بوده ام

نمی‌خواهم نگرانت کنم امّا
هنوز زنده‌ام
و این روزها هربار حواسم را پرت کرده‌ام در خیابان
بوق اولین ماشین، عقب‌عقبم رانده است

نمی‌خواهم نگرانت کنم امّا
این شب‌ها هربار
ناامیدی مرا به پشت بامِ خانه رسانده است
با احتیاط پله‌ها را
یکی
یکی

I need more memories with you
To build a nest egg for my old age
For the years
when a woman needs romantic memories more
    than her monthly stipend;
Like the missing button of your shirt,
Like your fingerprint on my glasses,
Like a lighter, a strand of hair, something…

Things I can examine later
And believe that some days
I had truly been alive
Truly,
A woman alive.

☙

I don't want to worry you, but
I am still alive and
these days
when I am distracted in the streets
the sound of the horn of the first car
makes me take a step back

I don't want to worry you, but
these nights
Whenever despair has lead me to the rooftop
Cautiously
One
by one

یکی
پایین آمده‌ام
با اینکه می‌دانستم در من
دیگر چیزی برای شکستن نمانده است

این شب‌ها روی پیشانی‌ام
جای روییدنِ شاخ می‌خارد و
پوستم این شب‌ها زبر و خشن شده است
و تو از شکوه کرگدن شدن چه می‌دانی؟

و بر این سیارهٔ خاکی موجوداتی هستند
که سرانجام فهمیده‌اند
بی‌عشق می‌شود زنده ماند
موجودات عجیبی
که بی‌آنکه کسی جایی نگرانشان باشد
با احتیاط از خیابان عبور می‌کنند
پله‌ها را دست به نرده پایین می‌آیند
و صبح‌ها در پارک می‌دوند
موجودات باشکوهی
که اگر خوب به سخت‌جانی چشم‌هایشان خیره شوی، می‌فهمی
هنوز نسل دایناسورها منقرض نشده است –

نمی‌خواهم نگرانت کنم
نمی‌خواهم نگرانت کنم امّا
امّا
نداشتنت را بلد شده‌ام
و مثل کودکی که سرانجام فهمیده است

by one
I have come down the stairs
Though I knew
Nothing unbroken remained within me

These nights
where the horn is growing
on my forehead
itches and
These days
my skin has become rough and dry and
What do you know of the splendor of morphing
   into a rhino?

And on this planet there are creatures
Who have finally understood
They can live without love;
Strange creatures
Who without worrying anyone
Cautiously cross streets
Hold the railing while coming downstairs
And run in the parks in the mornings

Splendid creatures
If you stare intently into their intense eyes,
You will understand that dinosaurs are not extinct

I don't want to worry you
I don't want to worry you, but...but...
I have learned to be without you
And like a child who has finally learned that

تمام آنچه در تاریکی‌ست
همان‌هاست که در روشنایی‌ست،
به خیانتِ دست‌های تو فکر می‌کنم
که تمام این سال‌ها
چراغ‌ها را
خاموش نگه داشته بودند.

ॐ

چندسال است
که وقتی می‌گویم باران
واقعاً منظورم باران است
وقتی می‌گویم پاییز،
واقعاً منظورم پاییز است
و وقتی به تو فکر می‌کنم،
واقعاً منظوری ندارم

چندسال است
که پاییزِ چسبیده به پنجره غمگینم نمی‌کند
از خواندن «عقاید یک دلقک» گریه‌ام نمی‌گیرد
و از عقب انداختن چیزی نگران نمی‌شوم

دیر است دیگر
آن‌قدر مرده‌ای که نگاهم از تو عبور می‌کند
و برای دوباره دیدنت
باید آن‌قدر به عقب برگردم،
تا نسلم منقرض بشود
باید
برسم به روزهایی

What exists in darkness
Is what exists in plain light
I reflect on the betrayal of your hands
Which all these years
Had kept the light
Off.

꩜

For several years
when I say rain,
I truly mean rain.
When I say autumn
I truly mean autumn.
and my thoughts of you
have no significance.

For several years now
Watching autumn so close to the window, doesn't
    make me sad
Reading a clown's ideas doesn't make me cry
And postponing things doesn't make me anxious

It's too late now
You are dead to me and I look through you
And to see you again
I must go as far back
As my generation's extinction
Back to days

که جایی
میان خون و خفا شروع به تپیدن کردم

من
یک قلب قدیمی‌ام
از آن‌هایی‌که سخت عاشق می‌شوند
از آن ساختمان‌های عجیبی‌که هرچه بیشتر می‌لرزند،
محکم‌تر می‌شوند
و یک‌روز می‌بینی به‌سختی می‌خندم
به‌سختی گریه می‌کنم
و این،
ابتدای سنگ‌شدن است

بی هیچ منظوری به تو فکر می‌کنم
و بی‌هیچ‌دلیلی متشکرم که دوباره پاییز است
متشکرم که هوا بارانی ست
و با این‌حال
حرف دوباره‌ای با تو ندارم

مثل دلقک بی‌دلیلی
با سنگی نهصدهزارماهه در سینه
که رقت‌انگیزترین هق‌هقش را بر چهره کشیده‌است
در پیاده‌روهای پاییزهای دوباره نشسته‌است
و برایش مهم نیست
سکه‌هایی‌که در کلاهش می‌اندازند،
تقلبی‌ست

surrounded by blood, hidden
when my heart started beating

I
Am an old-fashioned heart
One of those that falls hard
One of those strange buildings
that become stronger
the more they tremble
and one day you will see me barely laughing,
barely crying,
and thus starts the transformation to a rock.

I think of you with no particular purpose
With no apparent reason, I am grateful it's autumn again
I am grateful that it's rainy

and through it all
I have nothing to tell you

Like an aimless clown
with a nine hundred thousand month old rock on its chest
Who has painted the most heart wrenching sobs on his face
Is seated on the sidewalks of repeated autumns
who does not care
that the coins thrown in his hat
are all counterfeit.

دوستت دارم
و چقدر توضیح دادن
حرف های ساده
سخت است

۴۴

I love you
And how difficult it is
To explain
Simple utterances

Bita Malakuti

Date of Birth: 1973
Place of Birth: Tehran
Place of Residence: Czech Republic
Education: BA, Dramatic Arts, Azad University of Tehran
Profession: researcher, writer, poet
Books: Two collections of poetry

بادكنك ها

غربت جا يی است
در وطنم
آنجا
كه بادكنك ها
خاطرات تولد
نه،
شوخی كودكانه مرگ اند

Balloons

Exile is a place
in my country
where
the balloons
are not reminders of birth
But the juvenile banter of death!

به دیدنم بیا
پنهانی
مثل اولیس
مثل آن آخرین سرباز
که در کافه ی مرزی
منتظر است
می دانم
سرانجام
می بوسمت و تهران آزاد می شود

Come to me
Secretly
Like Ulysses
Like that last soldier
Waiting in the café
at the border
I know
Finally
I will get to kiss you
and
Tehran will be liberated!

Mandana Mashayekhi

Date of Birth: 1973
Place of Birth: Iran
Place of Residence: England
Education: PhD, Creative Writing, Newcastle University
Profession: instructor, poet
Books: one poetry collection

جامانده

چمدانم را می بندم:
آخرین بوسه تو
قطراتی از کارون
کلماتی از مولانا
چند نت از رعد و برقی که هنوز نزده
و مشتی از گرد آن جسدها
که هنوز چشم بندشان نپوسیده

Left Behind

I pack my suitcase:
Your last kiss
Drops from the Karun*
Words from Rumi
A few notes from the thunder that has not yet occurred
And a fistful of dust from those corpses
whose blindfolds have not yet rotted

---

*The longest and only navigable river in Iran, Karun thought by
some to be one of the rivers of Eden (the others being the Tigris and
the Euphrates).

با نوی بلند قد و سیاه پوشم منتظر است
بر می گردم از نیمه راه
بلیتم
در کشوی میز
جامانده.

۷

مادر

تلق تلق تلق
چرخ می چرخد به عادت
لیلا را دیروز بردند
احمد را فروردین
محمد را سال ها پیش
تلق تلق تلق
صدای زنگ دری نیست
گفتگویی نیست
تلق تلق تلق
می چرخد چرخ خیاطی به عادت

My tall lady in black is waiting
I return midway
My ticket
left behind
in the desk drawer

❧

Mother

Chuka chuka chuka
The wheel turns as usual
They took away Leila yesterday
And Ahmad in March
And Mohammad many years ago
Chuka chuka chuka
No sound of a door bell
No conversation
Chuka chuka chuka
The sewing machine turns as usual

❧

Shokooh Mirzadegi

Date of Birth: 1944
Place of Birth: [—]
Place of Residence: United States
Education: [—]
Profession: author, playwright, journalist, activist, poet
Books: one poetry collection

وقتی که سنگ عشق می خوریم

میان تازیانه و سنگ
میان آفتابگردان ها و آهوها
میان میدان ها، جمعیت، چراغ
تاب می خورم
از این سر جهان
به آن سر جهان
معلقم میان لحظه ی رفتن و آمدن
که مرا می بوسی
می گویم: چند دقیقه به ساعت مانده!
می گویی: جهان همین چند لحظه است
جهان همین چند لحظه است

When Stoned by Love

Between the whip and the stone
Between the sunflowers and the deer
Between the squares, the crowd, the traffic light
I swing
From this end of the world
To the other side of the world
I am suspended between arrival and departure
When you kiss me
I say: few minutes are left to the hour!
You say: the world is these few moments.

بگرد و ببین!
همان گونه که
در نقشه های قدیمی
می گردی
تا آن نقطه ی درخشان را
پیدا کنی.

مشتاق باش و ببین
هیچ لحظه ای گم نمی شود
درست مثل کلمه
مثل صدا
که از میانه ی خاك
و از میانه ی درخت و آسمان
بیرون می دود
و می نشیند میان دست هایت

****

جهان همین لحظه است
در همین نگاه آبی که اکنون
بر کف پایم
— درست زیر انگشت شصت چپم —
اشك می شود.

چرا جای شلاق هیچ وقت خوب نمی شود؟
چرا دوباره آن را نمی بوسی؟

نگاهت را برگردان!
جهان همین لحظه است
همین لحظه
که بر شقیقه های ما

The world is these few moments.
Look around and see!
The same way
you search in old maps
To find that bright spot

Be excited and see
No moment is lost
Just like a word
like voice
That from the depths of the earth
And from between the tree and the sky
Runs out
And sits in your hands

****

World is this very moment
In this very blue view
that on the sole of my foot
 – right under my left big toe –
Turns into a tear.

Why doesn't the trace of a whip ever heal?
Why don't you kiss it again?

Avert your gaze!
World is this very moment
This very moment
When red holes open

حفره هایی سرخ باز می شود
وقتی که سنگ عشق می خوریم
و بوسه هایمان آه می شود
و می میرد.

چرا خدا نمی داند سنگ چیست
و آواز باران
در هیاهوی سنگ ها گم می شود؟

چرا طبل همیشه می کوبد، گنگ
چرا صدای آرشه ها این همه هوشیارند
و چرا تنها وقتی عشق می آید
طبل ها ساکت می شوند؟

چرا این همه چرا
در همین لحظه ها شکل می گیرند
-همین لحظه های دیر یا زود

****

تاب می خورم
از این سر جهان
به آن سر جهان
به رد پای آهوها
بر علف های خشک نگاه می کنم.
جز تو به هیچ کس نگفته ام
که شب ها به آهوها
غذا می دهم
-وقتی که همسایه ها خوابند و
مأموران حفاظت از محیط زیست

On our temples
When we are stoned by love
And our kisses turn into sighs
And die.

Why doesn't God know what a stone is
Why does the rain's melody
Get lost in the clamor of stones?

Why does the drum always beat, mute
Why is the sound of the bows so alert
And why do the drums quiet down
Only when love arrives?

Why are so many whys
Shaped in these very moments
These moments, sooner or later

****

I swing
From this side of the world
To the other side of the world
And I look at the tracks of deer
At the dried grass.
I haven't told anyone but you
That I feed deer
Every night
 – when the neighbors are asleep
And wouldn't inform

را خبر نمی کنند.

کسی جز ما نمی داند

بر سُم آهوها

راز لحظه و شتاب حك شده است

همان که «بیجه» با خود داشت

-زنی که

در تاریخ گم شد و

فقط ما می دانیم کجاست

و رد نگاهش وابو ستاره ها

می شناسیم.

****

تاب می خورم

از این سر جهان

به آن سر جهان

و آخرین قطره ی باران را می نوشم

مست می شوم

و از خاك بر می خیزم.

آفتابگردان منم

و عطر شیرین آفتاب تویی

بر پوستم می نشینی

و زیبایی مسری ات

زیبایم می کند.

تاب می خورم

از این سر جهان

به آن سر جهان

و دست می کشم

برسرخانه ای که قرن هاست

The animal control officer.
Nobody but us remain
On deer's paws
The secret of moments and haste are engraved
The one that Bijeh* had on him
 – A woman who
Got lost in history and
We only know where she is
And recognize
The imprint of her gaze on the stars

****

I swing
From this side of the world
To the other side of the world
And I drink the last raindrop
And I get drunk
And rise from the earth.
I am sunflower
And you are the sweet scent of sunshine
You land on my skin
Any your contagious beauty
Renders me beautiful.
I swing
From this side of the world
To the other side of the world
And I touch up

---

* Nickname of a notorious Iranian serial killer

به آن سر نزده ام
اما هنوز می دانم
کجاست.
هنوز کلیدش در دست من است
و نشانی اش درچشم های تو.
آیا هنوز وقت بازگشت نیست؟

℘

ساعتم به وقت فرداست

هیچ چیز به آغاز باز نمی گردد جزعشق
که از نفس و
آسمان و
توحش گذشته است
که رنگ کهنگی ندارد
و در ذات خود
نامیراست.

یادت می آید؟
تنها با بوسه ای
از آسمان فرود آمدیم
و در وسعت زمین درخشیدیم؟

یادت می آید؟
آتش هایی را که از سنگ جوشیدند،
و گندم هایی که
در خون گوزن ها جوانه زدند؟

The house that I have not visited for centuries
But I still know
Where it is.
I still have its keys in my hand
And its whereabouts in your eyes
Is it still not time to return home?

My watch is set to tomorrow's time

Nothing returns to the beginning, except love
Which has gotten through breath
And sky
And fear
That's not colored by age
And is immortal
in its very nature

Do you remember?
With only a kiss
We descended from the sky
And shone in the vastness of the earth?

Do you remember
The fires that boiled from stone
And the wheat
That sprouted in the blood of the deer?

یادت می آید
کلیدهای نامریی سُل
آوازهای نا شنیده ه ی در پرواز
و رقص بی توقف ما را
از کرانه تا کرانه دریاها؟

یادت می آید
آنگاه که عقربه های نور
بر بستر ساعت های شنی
راز سر بسته زمان را
گشودند
و فردا در سینه ی ما شکفت؟

****

اکنون ساعتم به وقت فرداست
به وقت آفتابگردان هایی
که در کوچه ی خورشید ایستاده اند؛

ساعتم به وقت باغ های آفتابی
و پنجره هایی ست
که هرگز بسته نمی شوند–
بی هراس از توفان های گیج
و پرده های دلگیر؛

ساعتم به وقت آب هایی ست
که هر ثانیه از لبان ماهی می گذرند
و نیلوفرهایی
که در مهربانی برکه ها
تا دروازه های فیروزه می روند؛

Do you remember
The invisible Sol keys
The unheard songs in flight
And our nonstop dancing
From coast to coast?

Do you remember
When the hour hands of light
On the framed bed of hourglasses
Revealed the mystery of time
And the next day
a scream burst open in our chests

****

Nowadays, My watch is set to tomorrow's time
To the time of Sunflowers
Standing in the alley of the sun

My watch is set to the sunny orchards
To windows
That will never close
Fearless of meandering storms
And dingy curtains

My watch is set to the time of the waters
That pass through the fish's lips each second
And the water lilies
That with the kindness of ponds
Go to the turquoise gates;

ساعتم به وقت بوسه ای است
که قرن ها سفر کرده
تا بر تن آهو
و عطر دیوانه ی بیدها مهربان
بنشیند؛

ساعتم به وقت توست
به وقت سرزمینی که
مردانش با جثه های کوچك و لاغر
از دیوارهای سنگی می گذرند
و زنان شاعرشب
با گلوی پرنده سخن می گویند

چه ساعتی است آنجا؟
مگر ماه بر صخره نشسته
یا آفتاب از خیال دریا می گذرد
که خواب های رنگی ام
از خنده و اشتیاق پرشده اند؟

چه ساعتی است آنجا؟
که عقربه های ساعتم
با نورسفر می کنند،
و ستون های هزاران ساله
در عطر زندگی غوطه می خورند؟

چه ساعتی است آنجا؟

My watch is set to the kiss
That has traveled for centuries
To land on
the deer's body
And the mad scent of kind weeping willows;

My watch is set to your time
To the time of a land
Where its men with their small and thin stature
Pass by stone walls
And its women poets of the night
Speak through bird-like throats

What time is it there?
Has the moon sat on the rock
Or the sun passed through the sea's mind
That my colorful dreams
Are filled with joy and laughter?

What time is it there?
That the hands of my watch
Travel with the light,
and thousand year old pillars
float in the scent of life?

What time is it there?

Soheila Mirzaei

Date of Birth: 1964

Place of Birth: Urmia

Place of Residence: Germany

Education: BA, Clinical Psychology

Profession: social worker, author, poet, journalist, rock
  climbing instructor

Books: four poetry collections

گره

انگشت‌ات را بردار
در گلویم جای سکته‌ای می‌خارد
سرفه‌ات را بردار
تا در دل این کوچه باریک شوم
طناب طاقت این همه طول را ندارد
چارپایه بیفتد
روی هوا ماضی خواهم شد تا بعید
عقربه اوقاتم را می‌داند
حتا
وقتی حلقه‌ات انگشتم را بلعیده باشد

Knot

Remove your finger
A rupture in my throat itches
Take away your cough
So in the heart of this narrow sinister alley
The rope cannot bear such length
the stool can fall
In the air, I become the past, distant past
The clock hands know of my hours
Even
When your ring has devoured my finger

راه

چمدانی هستم
می روم از این شهر به آن شهر
تأخیرقطارها را تاب می آورم
بارانی که پایم را بالا می گیرد
دستی که به گلویم چفت می شود
پشت سایه ها متوقف شده ایم

از سرم صدا می ریزد
در تنم ساکن می شوی
شهرها دهکده ها رودها و کوه ها
جار می زنند که ساده ات کردیم
سال ها می ریزند روی گلهای پیراهنم
چروکشان از سن ام بالا می رود

قفل شده ام با رمزی که از خاطرت رفته است

چمدانی هستم
پر از چم و خم های رهگذران
پر از شیشه هایی که خرد شده اند در چشمانم

بوی سکوت مرطوبم کرده است
قطارها با تأخیرهم به مقصد نمی رسند
قول می دهم
پیش از آن که در خواب یك نفس بدوم تا نرسم
پشت پلك های راوی بیدار شوم

Road

I am a suitcase
I go from this city to the next
I tolerate the train delays
A rain that suspends my foot in midair
A hand that locks on my throat
We have been stopped behind the shadows

Noise pours out of my head
You inhabit my body
Cities, villages, rivers and mountains
Proclaim that we have rendered you simple
Years pour on the flowers of my dress
Their wrinkles advance my age

I have been locked with a code which you have forgotten

I am a suitcase
Filled with the knick knacks of the passer-bys
Filled with glasses broken in my eyes

The scent of silence has moistened me
Trains don't reach their destination even with delays
I promise
Before running nonstop, and not arriving, in my dream
I will wake up behind the narrator's eyelids

Sara Mohammadi Ardehali

Date of Birth: 1976
Place of Birth: Tehran
Place of Residence: Iran
Education: MA Sociology, Allameh Tabatabaei University
Profession: author, poet
Books: four poetry collections

ته چاه زندگی می کنم
چاهی خشك

بالایی ها
یا خبر ندارند
یا خودشان را می زنند به آن راه

سطل را
دست و دلبازانه
پرت می کنند پایین
می خورد به تاق سر من

I live at the bottom of a well
A dried well

Those above me
 are either not aware
Or pretend not to know

Generously
They throw down
The bucket
It hits me on the head

شاید هم انتظار دارند
در این تاریکی
بیشتر فرو بروم
و به آب برسم

چ

حُسن یوسف

به اخبار شامگاهی کاری ندارد
وقت آفتاب
برگ تازه می دهد
وسط برگ هایش شرابی،
کناره ها سبز.

چ

من و تو

بیچاره شمعدانی
این روزها که ناخوشم
دو سه برگش خشک شده
چه می شود کرد
لیوان آب ما یکی است

چ

Maybe they are waiting
That I sink further
In this darkness
And reach water

❧

Painted Nettle

It doesn't care about the evening news
When there is sunlight
It grows new leaves
The middle of the leaves wine-colored
The perimeter green

❧

You and I

Poor geranium
These days that I don't feel well
Two, three of its leaves have dried
What can we do
We drink from the same glass of water

❧

کار تمام وقت

هیچ مردی نمی خواهد
عاشق زنی شود
که در سیرک کار می کند

از آن زن ها که باید روی طناب راه بروند

عاشق زنی شود
که هر لحظه ممکن است سقوط کند
و اگر سقوط نکند
هزارها نفر برایش
کف می زنند

گردنبند

در تمام میهمانی ها
آویز گردن من
کلید خانه ی توست

حالا بگذریم
مرا جرأت آمدن نیست و
تو را
جرأت عوض کردن قفل

Full Time Job

No man wants
to fall in love with a woman
who works in the circus

One of those women who has to walk on a tightrope

To fall in love with a woman
Who may come crashing down at any moment
And if she does not crash
Thousands of people
Will applaud her

❧

Necklace

In all parties
My necklace
Is your house key

Forget it
I don't dare come over
You don't dare change the lock

Jila Mossaed

Date of Birth: 1948
Place of Birth: Tehran
Place of Residence: Sweden
Education: University of Jondi Shapur
Profession: author, poet, member of the Swedish Academy
Books: ten poetry collections in Persian

زن تمام روزها را
لباس می شست
جارو می کرد
اطو می کرد
ظرف می شست

و هر غروب

در شیشه ای دردار
آواز می خواند
به زبانی که هیچ کس نمی دانست

Every day the woman
Would wash the clothes
Sweep
Iron
Wash the dishes

And every evening

Into a glass with a lid
Would sing
In a language no one understood

سپس
در شیشه رامی بست
به رختخواب می رفت
تنها بود

࿇

عشق

ملافه های سکوت را
تا می کنم برای روزهایی
که صدا غایب است
عشق لباس ترس پوشیده
و خود را در جایی گم کرده است

سکوت شکل پذیر است
می ریزد
جمع می شود
پهن می شود
کارد می شود
می برّد
پنهان می شود
گول می زند
می میرد
بیدار می شود
می رقصد

Then
She would close the lid
Go to bed
She was alone

❧

Love

I fold the sheets of silence
For the days
That voice is absent
That love is cloaked in fear
And has gotten lost somewhere

Silence is malleable
It pours
cleans up
Spreads
Turns into a knife
Cuts
Hides
Tricks
Dies
Wakes up
Dances

بی صدا لبه ی بیداری می ایستد
و قلب ام را از درون
غلغلک می دهد

سکوت دوست من است
ملافه می شود
آغوش می شود
آرام ام می کند.

۶

پایانِ من

دهان شب از پولك آغشته است
بازدم عشق
تنهایی ست
من در خیابان هایی که به هم گره خورده اند
نا پدید شده ام
و الفبای هیچ زبا نی را نمی دانم
در آسانسوری که به اعماق می رود
آیینه ای نصب است
که شیارهای روح را نشان می دهد
من پنج قارۀ جهان را خالی دیدم
و از بیشه ای که بر آسمانخراشی
باقی مانده بود
علفی چیده ام
که همهُ پیامبران آینده را
مسموم می کند

۶

Silently stands on the brink of wakefulness
And tickles my heart
From the inside

Silence is my friend
It turns into a sheet
It turns into an embrace
It calms me down.

❧

The End of Me

Night's mouth is soaked in sequins
Love's exhalation is
loneliness.
I have disappeared
in streets that are knotted together and
I don't know the alphabet of any language
In an elevator descending to the depths
A mirror is installed
Which shows the grooves of the soul
I saw the five continents of the world empty
And from a thicket
remaining
On a skyscraper
I picked an herb
that would poison
all future prophets

❧

رها یم

از شما دور می شوم
به سوی دره خم نمی شوم
از آن فراز اثیری
به اعماق
نگاه نمی کنم
شما دره اید
شما حفره اید
شما از خود تهی یا نید
حتی صدای مرا می دزدید
از شما دور می شوم
ذره ام
با باد یکی شده ام
نام و تبار از آن شما
من وزنده ام
از پنج حس ناقص انسانی
اختاپوس شیاد درد
رهایم
از شما دور می شوم
تا آنسوی دیوارهای درک
آنقدر کوچکم
که دیگرهیچ خدایی
مرا به جد نمی گیرد

I Am Free

I distance myself from you
I don't lean towards the valley,
From that ethereal height
I don't look
to the depths
You are hollows
You are holes
You are devoid of your selves
You even steal my voice
I distance myself from you
I am a particle
I have become one with the wind
You can keep your name, your lineage
I am the wind
I am free of
The five imperfect human senses
The treacherous octopus of pain
I distance myself from you
To the other side of walls of understanding
I am so small
That no God
Will take me seriously any longer

❧

ساده

نه ستارگان
خواب زندگی ام را دیده بودند
و نه جباری به نام خدا
هستی ام را
در ما ورای حزن
رقم زده بود
من طعمه تخیل انسانم
افسانه به همین سادگی است

به زن

این سر توست
با دو زلف بلند بافته
این فرق سر توست

حنایی ست
زعفرانی ست
زخمی ست
بوی گل می دهد
سر تو میان خواب من چه می کند
سر تو که از ضربه ی دست مرد
هنوز دوران دارد
نصف شب است
صورتت را گم کرده ام
مادر منی

Simple

Neither the stars
had imagined my life
Nor an almighty God
Had figured my existence
in the depths of sorrow
I am prey to human imagination
The tale is this simple

೩

To Woman

This is your head
With two long braids
This is the part of your hair
Henna Colored
Saffron Colored
Wounded
Flower scented
What is your head doing in the midst of my dreams?
Your head still dizzy
from a man's blow
It is midnight
I have lost your face
You are my mother

مادر مادر مادران منی
تو نشانم می دهی
من نگاه می کنم
پسری هفت ساله
در خوابم را می کوبد
با انگشتان پینه بسته ی هفتاد سالگان
و چشمان روشنش را گرو می گذارد
در برهوت خواب من
شما چه می کنید
هر شب

❧

You are the mother of the mother of my mothers
You point
I look
A seven year old boy
Knocks on the door of my dream
With the callused fingers of septuagenarians
And he pawns his bright eyes
In the desert of my dream
What do you do
every night?

Granaz Moussavi

Date of Birth: [—]
Place of Birth: Tehran
Place of Residence: Australia
Education: PhD Candidate, University of Western Sydney
Profession: literary critic, film director, screenwriter, poet
Books: five poetry collections

شاعر

لحظه های کوچکم را در دستانت بگیر
تقویم من از تاریخ خالی و از حادثه پراست
سلول های انفرادی ام را از تنت بتکان
می خواهم در مبلی که می نشینی
در فرش گل گلی ات
در پرده که آسمان را دور می کند
در تنت که ویزا نمی دهد و
از پناهندگی ام لب پر می زند
منتشر شوم
مجوز نگیرم و
دست به دست دور میدانهایت بگردم

Poet

Hold my brief moments in your hands
My calendar is devoid of dates and filled with incidents
Shake out my solitary cells from your clothes
I want to permeate
The armchair where you sit
Your flowered carpet
The curtain that keeps the sky at a distance
Your body that denies me an entry visa
And is overflowing with my refugee status.
Without permission
Hand in hand, I want to circle your roundabouts

زیر زمینی پخش شوم درثانیه هایت
و هی مدام سر تا ته بخوانیم
زیرحرفهای معمولیم خط بکشی
دوره ام کنی
تمامم کنی
و دوباره هی منتشر شوم

؏

رابطه

نشسته ام زیر پای علف
من سبز می شوم
او
از راه بدر

؏

صدا می افتد
و آهی سبزدر هوا تکرار می شود
انگار نه انگار
زیر پای حنجره هامان
از چارپایه و هر چیز دیگری خالی است

Clandestinely, I want to infiltrate your every second
I want you to read me from cover to cover repeatedly
To underline my ordinary words
To review me
To complete me and
I reissue everything yet again.

Relationship

Seated at the foot of the grass
I sprout
He
Loses his way

Voice falls
And a green sigh in the air repeats
As if
Underneath our voice boxes
There are no stools
And no other objects either

Sepideh Nikroo

Date of Birth: 1984
Place of Birth: Tehran
Place of Residence: Tehran
Education: MA Persian Literature
Profession: Children and young adults author and poet
Books: Four collections of poetry

نبودن تو

نبودن هواست

نبودن گرما در اوج یخبندان

نبودن آب

در صحرای بی پایان

نبودن عشق

در مدرنیسم کلافه ی خیابان

معشوق قد بلند من

مَرد!

در دست های تو می شود زن بود

زنده بود

Your absence

is the absence of oxygen

The absence of heat

in the freezing cold

The absence of water

in the vast desert

The absence of love

in the stifled modernism of the street

My tall beloved Man!

In your hands, one can be a woman

Be alive

و هر چیز جز نبودن تو
سهل است
سخت نیست

❧

شیارهای گوشه‌ی چشمانت
خطوط پر تلاطم دریاست
التهاب رفتن و آمدن
التهاب بوسیده‌شدن
با چشم‌های بسته
انتظار لحظه‌ی لمس لبانی
که مثل اولین قطره‌ی باران
نامنتظرانه اوج خوشبختی‌ست

شیارهای گوشه‌ی چشمانت
فردای نیامده است
امید خندیدن در نور مهتاب
آن لحظه‌ی بی قراری
که پرستار می‌گوید متولد شد
و صدای زندگی از پشت دری بسته شنیده می‌شود

شیارهای گوشه‌ی چشمانت
التیام زخم‌های گذشته است
آن لحظه ای که...
که دیگر به خاطر نمی‌آورم

❧

and everything but your absence
is easy
It's not difficult!

❧

The laugh lines around your eyes
Are turbulent waters of the sea
The excitement of arrivals and departures
The excitement of being kissed with eyes closed
Awaiting the moment when lips touch
Like the first drop of rain
Unexpectedly
the epitome of happiness!

The laugh lines around your eyes
the tomorrows, yet to come
The hope of laughing under the moonlight
That restless moment
When the nurse announces birth
the sound of life heard from behind a closed door

The laugh lines around your eyes
the healing of wounds of the past
That moment when...
I no longer recall

❧

کنار من که نشسته ای
باد آرام می گیرد
گنجشک گم شده به لانه بر می گردد
و ابر کوچک سرگردان
سر به شانه ی کوه می نهد

آفتابی تو
هر جا که باشی
ساقه ام را به خود می کشی

৯

رنگ

رنگ قرمز
معنا دارد
رنگ لباس تو
وقتی به مهمانی می‌روی
معنا دارد
رنگ چشم‌های تو وقتی گریسته‌ای
معنا دارد
وقتی پرچم کشوری
می‌گرید
وقتی خیال تو
لحظه‌ها را گلوله می‌زند
معنا دارد

خون تو این سنگفرش را
تر کرده‌است

৯

When you sit next to me
The wind calms down
The lost sparrow
returns to the nest
the small, drifting cloud
leans on the mountain

You are sunshine
Wherever you are
You draw my stem towards you

❧

Color

The color red
is significant
The color of the dress
you wear to the party
is significant
The color of your eyes
after crying
is significant
When a country's flag
cries,
When your thought
shoots bullets at the moments
It's significant

Your blood
Is wet on the cobblestones

❧

وقتي که خوابیده
دیگر امیدي نیست
چیزی بگوید

تاریخ، تکان خورده
مثل جغرافیا پس از برخورد بزرگ
مثل مردمک چشم او و در آن پیشامدِ بزرگ
مثل حالتِ گوشه‌های لب‌هایم
در آن لحظه‌ی بزرگ

وقتی که پرنده رفته
دیگر امیدی نیست
که راهش را به خانه بازبیابد
هرچند بخواهد

&

اشتیاق

خورشیدِ بی‌پایان
می‌تابد بر من و تو
بر سقف خانه و فرودگاه
یکسان!

When he[*] is asleep
there's no hope
That he'll say something

History, shaken
like geography after the giant-impact[†]
Like the pupil of his eye at that great incident
Like the corner of my lips at that grand moment

Once the bird has flown away
There is no hope
That it will find its way back home
Even if it wants to.

❧

Eagerness

The eternal sun
shines on you and me
on the roof of the house and the airport
equally!

---

* There is a single subject pronoun for the third person singular
in Persian. "He" and "she" are both designated by "او" in Persian.
When there is no other indication, as in this poem, either "he" or
"she" could be inferred.

† Refers to the giant-impact hypothesis, which suggests that the
Moon formed from the ejecta of a collision between the proto-Earth
and a Mars-sized planet, approximately 4.5 billion years ago.

اما سایه‌ها یکسان نیست
سایه‌ی مردی ایستاده
پرشور
منتظر
با قلبی که در سایه نمی‌گنجد

و زنی
که دراز کشیده روی سایه‌اش
ناآرام
منتظر
با قلبی فشرده که سخت می‌تپد

خورشید تابیده یکسان
بر رفتن تو
بر ماندن من

But shadows are not the same
That of a man standing
Eager
Awaiting
with a heart not contained by the shadow

And a woman
who lies on her shadow
Restless
Awaiting
with a clenched heart, beating fast

The sun has shone equally
On your leaving
And my staying.

Partow Nooriala

Date of Birth: 1948
Place of Birth: Tehran
Place of Residence: United States
Education: MSW, Social Work Management; BA
  Philosophy & Psychology
Profession: writer, literary critic, publisher, and poet
Books: six poetry collections

نسیم خاطره

در نیمه‌های شب
بی‌خوابی، به ایوان میکشانَدَم؛
جنگلی مه‌آلود در برابرم
همهمه‌ی گُنگِ دریا، پسِ پشتِ جنگل

پَرِ پروازِ پرنده‌ای ناشناس، در شب
نسیم خاطره می‌پاشَد
بر بوسه‌ها
و نوازش‌ها

The Breeze of Memory

In the middle of the night
Insomnia dragged me to the balcony
A foggy forest before me
the muted tumult of the sea, beyond the deep forest

Flight of an unknown bird at night
sprinkles the breeze of memory
on kisses and caresses.

نخستین پرتو خورشید
دلِ تاریکی را می‌شکافد؛
به دَمی، همهمهٔ دور دریا
غوغای عبور آدم‌ها و ماشین‌هاست
و جنگل انبوه
درختانِ بی‌برگ و بار پائیزی

تنها حقیقت
دیوار سیمانیِ سرای سالمندان است
که سرد و خاکستری
از آن میان، سَرَک می‌کشد.

৵

باغ آبی

دورِن آب،
زنی جاریست.
درونِ آب،
صدای مکرّری مَوّاج است.
درونِ آب،
گیاهی عجیب می‌روید.
و در نهایت امواج
زیر دریاها
باغی است که هر غروب
زنی برفگون،
میان غنچهٔ گیلاس
و عطر مرموز یاس

The first ray of sunshine
Cleaves the heart of darkness
In an instant, the distant sea waves turn into
The deafening hubbub of humans and cars
And the dense forest
Leafless, fruitless autumnal trees.

The only truth
The cement wall of the nursing home
That cold and gray
Pokes its head out in the midst of all this.

❧

Water Garden

In the water
A woman flows.
In the water
A sound repeats in the waves.
In the water
A strange plant grows.
And at the height of the waves
Under the seas
There is a garden where a woman
White as snow,
Between cherry blossoms
And the mysterious scent of jasmines

گردش می کند،
و دسته گلها یی می چیند
به یاد روشنی ی
آب وُ آفتاب بهار،
و به عاشقانش
بخشش می کند.

۞

آفتاب گردان

رویایت
ظلمت را می رمانَد.

به دنبال آفتاب
سَمتِ تو می گردم؛
طلای گلبرگ وُ
شفای حضور.
کوبش منقار پرنده ای
بر سبزْدانه هام
از خواب
بیدارم می کند.

ﷺ

Strolls,
And picks bunches of flowers
In memory of a light
Water and the spring sun,
And lavishes them upon
her lovers.

Sunflower

Dreaming of you
Chases darkness away.

Following the sunlight
I turn to you
The gold of petals and
The cure of presence.
The pecking of a bird
At my green seeds
Wakes me
From my sleep.

Maryam Raeesdana

Date of Birth: 1967
Place of Birth: Tehran
Place of Residence: United States
Education: BA French, Tehran University
Profession: author, translator, poet
Books: one poetry collection

الهه ی بلور

چه رازی ست میان توو یاد کودکی
راهی کجا هستی؟
چه رازی ست میان توو عشق مهجور مانده
راهی کجا هستی؟
چه رازی ست میان تو و آرزوی از دست رفته
راهی کجا هستی؟
چه رازی ست میان تو و وطن نابود شده؟
راهی کجا هستی؟
چه رازی ست میان تو و مرگ
راهی کجا هستی؟

Crystal Goddess

What is the secret between you and childhood memories?
Where are you headed?
What is the secret between you and deserted love?
Where are you headed?
What is the secret between you and lost hope?
Where are you headed?
What is the secret between you and the destroyed homeland?
Where are you headed?
What is the secret between you and death?
Where are you headed?

ای اشك، الهه ی بلور
با من بگو
راهی کجا هستی؟

۶

می بینمت، پرنده
پر می کشی
به سوی آسمانت.
در سکوت درخت
شنیده می شوی.

۶

دشوار است،
هر صبح بر می‌خیزد،
به پرنده گوش می‌دهد.
سایه هایی که می‌آیند و می‌روند،
و بعد هیچ.
دشوار است
ادامه دادنِ این هیچ...

۶

O tear, crystal goddess
Tell me
Where are you headed?

I see you, bird
You spread your wing
Toward your sky.
In the silence of the tree
You are heard.

It's difficult
Every morning he wakes up,
Listens to the bird.
The shadows that come and go,
And then nothing.
It's difficult
To continue this nothing…

Nazanin Rahimi

Date of Birth: 1972
Place of Birth: Tehran
Place of Residence: Tehran
Education: BA, Dramatic Arts
Profession: literary critic, poet
Books: eight poetry collections

گلدان گل کوهی
با خزه ی انبوهی پوشانده شده بود
گلدان پشت پنجره ام
با خیال...
دو سه تکه ابر باران زا
قایقی بادبانی میان ابرها
کمی خورشید لای در مانده
قاب عکس مادر
شاخه های بیرون زده راش
چمدان قدیمی پدر
و پرنده ی مهاجر
آخرین باز مانده ی دوست داشتن

Pot of wildflowers
had been densely covered with moss
The flowerpot on my window sill
with imagination...

Two or three rain clouds
A sailboat among the clouds
A ray of sunshine through the door
Mother's picture in a frame
Branches of beech tree poking out
Father's old suitcase
And a migrant bird
The last survivor of love

این روزها
گلدان پای پنجره ام
با خیال

৵

به من بگو
هنوز بالای سر ما رودخانه جاری می شود
بگو که دست ها برای رسیدن به هم
اطلسی می شوند
چشم ها وابسته ی شمعدانی
و آغوش ها تنگاتنگ هم
برای لانه ی سهره ی که آوازش را
از دست داده است
من برای رسیدن به تو آهسته شدم
می دانی؟
شهر شیشه ای است
همه ی ما دیده می شویم
اما خوانده نمی شویم
ما خوانده نمی شویم

৵

هر روز
هزار دختر را بغل می کنم
به هوایی که
یکی از آنها تو باشی
دخترم...

These days
The flowerpot on my window sill
with imagination…

❧

Tell me
That the river still flows above us
Tell me that hands turn into petunias
To reach one another
Eyes fixed on geraniums
And tight embraces
For the nest of the goldfinch who has lost its song
I have slowed down to reach you
Do you know?
The city is made of glass
We can all be seen
But we cannot be read
We cannot be sung

❧

Everyday
I hug a thousand girls
Hoping that
You be
One of them
My daughter…

Nasrin Ranjbar Irani

Date of Birth: 1955
Place of Birth: Shiraz
Place of Residence: Germany
Education: PhD, Hamburg University
Profession:poet
Books: two poetry collections

من از تبار گلم، نام من گواه من است
بهاریم و همین بدترین گناه من است

خزان عدوی من است، خوب خوب می دانم
به کام خصم شکفتن، نه رسم و راه من است

ولی ز دوست نگردم، به جان دوست قسم
و این، مرام همیشه، نه گاهگاه من است

I'm of the ilk of flowers, my name is my witness[*]
We are spring flowers, and this is my worst sin

Fall is my enemy, I know it all too well
Blooming at the enemy's whim is not my practice

But I won't turn away from a friend, I vow on my
    friend's life
This is my constant, not occasional, principle

---

[*] The poet's first name, Nasrin, is also the Persian name of a
fragrant yellow flower of the narcissus family, jonquil or rush
daffodil.

به باغ می سپرم رنگ و بو اگر چه خزان
کمین نشسته و پی جوی اشتباه من است

دلم خوش است که از نوبهار می آید
امید رستن گلهای نو، پناه من است

من از تبار گلم، نام من گواه من است

❧

باران عشق که می بارد
چتر سکوت را می بندم
و زیر باران
به زندگی می زنم
تا گنجشکك پر گوی شعر را
در گریبانم
پناه دهم

خشکسال عشق که باشد
روی ایوان خاطره
می نشینیم
و ترکهای قلبم را
می شمارم

❧

I bestow the scent and color to the garden
Though fall is lurking and waiting for me to slip

I am delighted that spring will come again
Hope of new flowers blooming, that's my refuge

I am of the ilk of flowers, my name is my witness

❧

When love rains
I close the umbrella of silence
And under the rain
I live fully
To provide shelter, under my collar,
to the little talkative sparrow of poetry

When there is a drought of love
I sit
in the terrace of my memories
And I count
The fractures in my heart

❧

چیزی بگو!
با کلامی
ستاره ای
از آسمانی
می افتد.
و با کلامی
شاخه نرگس تنهایی
در شنزاری
میروید

چیزی بگو!

چیزی بگو
تا شهاب ها و نرگس ها
روزگارشان را بدانند
چیزی بگو
تا بمیرم
یا
برویَم

Say something!
With a word
A star falls
from the sky
And with a word
A lonely daffodil
grows
in the sand

Say something!

Say something
so that daffodils and shooting stars
know their fate
Say something
so that I die
Or
I grow

Fatima Ranjbari

Date of Birth: 1980

Place of Birth: Urmia

Place of Residence: Iran

Education: [—]

Profession: poet, editor

Books: one poetry collection

بی‌غم‌گسار، بی‌کس و تنها، غریب من
از خنده‌هایِ از تهِ دل بی‌نصیب من
از دشمنانِ جا شده در رختِ دوستی
هم خورده خون دیده و دل، هم فریب من
با زخم‌های واقعی‌ام خو گرفته‌ام
بیزارم از دروغِ دوا و طبیب من
هم‌دستِ هرکه بال و پرم را نشانه کرد
در کشتنِ پرندگی‌ام بی‌رقیب من
تن‌خورده‌ء حقارتِ آغوش‌های چرک
سرخورده از تحمل هر نانجیب من
مصداقِ خواستن نتوانستنم، ببین!
بی‌خستگی دویده، ولی در نشیب من

۳

Alone, lonesome, forlorn, stranger, that's me
Lacking the ability to belly laugh, that's me!
With enemies in friends' clothing
Tearful, heartbroken, betrayed, that's me!
Used to my deep, real wounds
Fed up with the lies of medicines and doctors,
    that's me!
An accomplice to whoever aims at my wings and
    feathers
Unmatched in killing my own flight, that's me!
Repulsed by the contact of filthy embraces
Dejected from putting up with every indecency,
    that's me!
 Behold the instance of my desire & impotence
Having run tirelessly, yet declining, that's me!

طنابِ دار، دستِ توست: حلقه دورِ گردنم

جهنم، آتشِ تنت؛ که سوخت در تبش، تنم

لبِ تو طعمِ زهر و تازیانه‌ی نوازشت

به ساقه‌های تُردِ من که شاخه‌شاخه بشکنم

قلمرو حقیرِ تو: اتاقِ خوابِ مشترک

کنیزِ مُهْر بر لبِ خلیفه‌ای که تو، منم!

نه در گذشته‌های بد که از همیشه تا اَبَد

پناهم از تویی که دوست، به شانه‌های دشمنم

منی که نان‌خورِ پدر؛ به نرخِ شیرِ مادرم

زمینِ بارور شدم؛ که باغِ نُطفه، دامنم

به سخت‌جانیِ سگم؛ بزن به سنگ‌ها مرا

بزن که بندِ مادری، بریده پای رفتنم

☙

جانش زده از جهانِ تو بیرون

پرواز که در قفس نمی‌گنجد

دریاست و جا نمی‌شود در تُنگ

عشقش به تنِ هوس نمی‌گنجد

Your hand, a noose, around my neck
Your body heat, hell, my body burnt by its fever

Your lips taste like poison, your caress feels like
    lashes
my fragile stems, breaking me branch by branch

Your despicable fiefdom, our shared bedroom
A tight-lipped slave, you are my master!

Not only in the horrid past, always and forever
I seek shelter from you, friend, on the shoulders of
    my foe

A dependent of my father, indebted to my mother's
    milk
I became fertile ground, my lap, a garden of seeds

I can doggedly endure; knock me down on the
    rocks
Strike me as the shackles of motherhood have
    prevented my escape

❧

Her being has surpassed your world
As flight cannot be confined to the cage
She's a sea and does not fit in a pitcher
Her love cannot be confined to carnal desire

دیگر به هرآنچه هست راضی نیست
زن سقفِ پر از تَرَک نمی‌خواهد
تنگ آمده در قفس نفس‌هایش
جان‌کندنِ مشترک نمی‌خواهد

৵

ای رفته از دل، رفته از خاطر!
افتاده طعمت از دهانِ من
صدها سخن دارم، ولی بگذار
ناگفته مانَد داستانِ من

৵

تو سال‌ها با سایه‌ها همدست
در کشتنِ خورشیدهای من
من با خودم بی رحم تر از تو
من با تو هم پیمان در این کشتن

৵

No longer satisfied with the status quo
She does not want a ceiling full of cracks
breathless in the cage
She no longer wants shared agony

You! No longer in my heart, no longer in my memory!
My mouth no longer likes your taste
I have hundreds of things to say but
Let my story remain untold

For years, you, accomplice of shadows
in the killing of my suns
And I, myself, even crueler than you,
am your ally in this killing

Mehrangiz Rassapoor (M. Pegah)

Date of Birth: 1952
Place of Birth: [—]
Place of Residence: England
Education: BA, Literature
Profession:literary critic, translator, poet
Books: four poetry collections

بسیاری جمع را مپندار مَحَك
چون جمع در اشتباه باشد بی شك
بر پیکره ی مذاهب و باورها
بنگر که همه پر از شکاف است و ترك

༄

در ذهن شود صفات انسانی پست
خوش آنکه به یُمن عشق، زین دام برست
ابله تر از او نباشد اندر عالم
کو در قفس است، با کلیدش در دست

༄

Don't take the size of a group as a touchstone
The crowd is undoubtedly wrong
Look at the corpus of beliefs and religions
Replete with cracks and gaps

❧

Humanity becomes ignoble in the mind
Blessed is one who escapes this trap through love
There's no one in the world more foolish
Than the one in the cage with the key in hand

❧

بر خویش دمی نظر نمایی گر تو
بینی همه چیز آید از تو، بر تو
دست از سر دیگران اگر برداری
دانی که بهشت هست و جهنم در تو

نوروز که سبز رنگ و سرخ أست و سپید
باز آمده با جامه رنگین امید
این جشن طبیعت است، می نوش و برقص
جزئی ز طبیعتیم ما، بی تردید

If you take the time to look at yourself
You'll see you cause all that happens to you, yourself
If you leave others out of this calculus
You'll know heaven and hell reside within yourself.

Nowruz with its green, red and white colors
Has returned with its colorful cloak of hope
It's nature's celebration: drink and dance
We're all a part of nature, no doubt!

Fatemeh Salarvand

Date of Birth: 1973
Place of Birth: Lorestan
Place of Residence: Tehran
Education: [—]
Profession: editor, commentator, and poet
Books: Four poetry collections.

رها کن این زن دیوانه را به حال خودش
دلش برای تو و غصه هاش مال خودش

رها کن این زن دیوانه را که معلوم است
به دست خویش کمر بسته بر زوال خودش

زنی که آمده از سرنوشت سیب و فریب
خودش جواب خودش! نه! خودش سوال خودش!

زنی که "هیچ مگوی"و زنی که "هیچ مپرس"
زنی مخاطب آواز های لال خودش

Leave this crazy woman to herself
Her heart is yours and her sorrow hers

Leave this crazy woman, it's clear
she is intent on destroying herself

A woman, whose fate comes from an apple and a ruse
She is her own answer! No! Her own question!

A woman, of the ilk of "Don't speak" and "Don't ask"
A woman, the audience of her own silent songs

زنی به تردی آیینه، سنگ تر از سنگ
شبیه بغض هزاران هزار سال خودش

زنی که هیچ به رویای آسمان نرسید
زنی پرنده که پوسید زیر بال خودش!

ع

سنگ خواهم شد مپرس از من سؤالی بعد از این
غیر خاموشی ندارم شرح حالی بعد از این

سرد و ساکت، زیستن در هیأت سنگین سنگ
سنگ آری...با دهان و چشم لالی بعد از این

نه سری دارم، نه سودایی، نه جانی نه دلی
نه غمی، نه آرزویی نه خیالی بعد از این

خاطرت آسوده باشد، چون که می بینی مرا
بی شکایت، بی سر سوزن ملالی بعد از این

سنگم و از خوابهایم باغ سبزی می دمد
در جهان دیگری، شاید مجالی بعد از این

ع

A woman, fragile as a mirror, hard as a rock
Resembling the millenia-old lump in her throat

A woman never reaching the dream of flight
A woman, a bird decayed under its own wing

꙾

I will turn into stone, ask me no questions from now on
Other than silence, I have nothing to share from now on

Cold and quiet, fossilized, living in the form of a stone
Like a stone, closed lips and eyes from now on

I have no thoughts, no passion, no soul, no heart
No sorrow, no wish, no dream from now on

Don't worry when you see me
No complaints, nor the slightest sadness from now on

I am a stone, a green garden grows in my dreams
In another world, a new arena from now on

꙾

عمری به دنبال تو گشتم بین عابرها
در کوچه ها و جاده ها، بین مسافرها

گشتم به دنبال تو هر سو ردّپایی بود
در آسمان، روی زمین، بین مهاجرها

مثل کبوتر پر کشیدم روی هر گنبد
گم شد دلم در جستجویت بین زائرها

از دوری ات سوزاندی ام طوری که می سوزد
حتی به حالم–ای مسلمان–حال کافرها!

دیوانه ام هرگز نبودی...خوب می دانم
حالا مرا دیوانه می خوانند شاعرها

৵

با کتاب و شعر
با ترانه، ساز
با آواز
با دوات و رنگ و نقاشی
با خطوط و ترمه و اسلیمی و کاشی
حال من جور است
نسبتم با هر چه جز این‌ها
نسبتاً دور است

৵

For a lifetime, in alleys, on roads,
among passersby and travelers
I searched for you

Wherever there were footprints
in the sky, on earth, among immigrants
I searched for you

Like a dove flying over every dome
My heart lost, among pilgrims
I searched for you

O Moslem!
With our separation you hurt me so,
that even non-moslems feel for me

You were never crazy about me,
I know it well
Nowadays the poets call me crazy

⚘

With a book and a poem
With a melody, a musical instrument
With a song
With an inkwell and color and drawing
With lines and termeh and arabesque and tile
I feel a connection
With everything but these, my connection
Is rather distant

⚘

تابستان

رود از شدت گرما به خودش می‌پیچد
دشت تب‌دار است
نه نسیمی می‌آید نه کسی
خبری از باران دارد
حتی
خود تابستان هم
دارد از هُرمِ نفس‌های خودش می‌سوزد

❧

اگرچه با دل من مَحرم اند این کلمات
برای از تو سرودن کم اند این کلمات

تمام آنچه که دارم، گمان مبر ای خوب!
تمام آنچه که می خواهم اند این کلمات

گل منی و برایت چقدر ناچیزند
اگر چه مثل گل مریم اند این کلمات

برای آن که به نامت شبیه تر باشند
حریر و اطلس و ابریشم اند این کلمات

تو را به یاد من آورده اند از این روست
عزیزتر ز همه عالم اند این کلمات

Summer

In the scorching heat, the river is doubled over
The plain is feverish
No breeze
Not a soul with hope for rain
Even the summer itself
Is burning by the heat of its own breath

⁓

Though familiar with my heart are these words
Meager for a poem about you, are these words

With all that I have, don't surmise my dear
All that I want are these words

You are my flower, yet insignificant for you
Though, like tuberose flowers are these words

To better resemble your name
Organza, satin and silk are these words

They have reminded me of you and thus
More precious than anything in this world, are
   these words

چقدر چشم به راه صدات بنشینم؟
بیا که بی تو سراسر غم اند این کلمات!

۶

پرنده باشم و از آسمان جدا باشم؟
فقط به قدر قفس خواستی رها باشم؟

پرنده باشم و بالم به ابرها نخورد؟
به دام و دانه ی این خاک مبتلا باشم؟

دلم چگونه نلرزد برای آبی ها
اسیر خط خطی میله ها چرا باشم؟

چقدر قیچی و سنگ و چقدر قیچی و سنگ
شکسته بال بمانم همیشه تا باشم؟

گلوی تُرد من از شور واژه لبریز است
نگفته بودی خاموش و بی صدا باشم!

به من بگو که نباشم، به من بگو که بمیر
ولی نخواه که از آسمان جدا باشم!

۶

How long shall I await the sound of your voice?
Come, in your absence, sorrowful are these words!

❧

To be a bird away from the sky?
You wanted me free within a cage?

To be a bird, my wings not reaching the clouds?
Addicted to traps and seeds on the earth?

How not to worry about the skies
Why should I be imprisoned behind bars?

Scissor, rock and scissor, rock, for how long?
Remain forever broken-winged only to exist?

My fragile throat, filled with a passion for words
You hadn't told me to be silent and voiceless!

Tell me not to be, tell me to die
But don't ask me to stay away from the sky!

❧

با تو همراهند، اما همرهانت نیستند
همنشینانی که از جنس جهانت نیستند

داستان غربت است و"قصّه ای پرآبِ چشم"
همدلانت نه...که حتی همزبانت نیستند

نه شریك غصّه هایت، نه شریك شادی ات
این رفیقان جز شریك آب و نانت نیستند

می شناسندت به نام و ناشناسی بین شان
آشنایانند و دنبال نشانت نیستند

روزِ سختی را نمی دانم که هم امروز نیز
جز نمك بر زخم های استخوانت نیستند

کاشکی نامهربانی را بلد بودی کمی!
مهربانی...حیف اما مهربانت نیستند

سهل باشد دشمنی از دشمنان دیدن ولی
درد دارد دوستانت دوستانت نیستند

౸

They accompany you, but are not your allies
They are companions, not of your world's fabric

It's the tale of exile and a "tale filled with tears"*
Like-minded, not!...not even speaking the same
    language!

They don't share your sorrow, they don't share your joy
These friends only share your bread and salt

They know your name, but you remain unknown
    among them
They're acquaintances, not interested in who you are

Even today, let alone difficult days,
Except as salt rubbed into your deepest wounds, they
    don't exist

I wish you knew how to be unkind...even if a little bit!
You are kind! Alas, your kindness is not returned

It's easy to witness animosity from enemies but
It's painful when your friends are not true friends

                    ❧

_____

* This is a reference to the birth of Sohrab, Rostam and Tahmineh's
son, in "The Tale of Sohrab," in Ferdowsi's *Shahnameh*. The story goes
on to depict Sohrab's battles, including the one where he faces his
father, Rostam. In this battle, Rostam unknowingly mortally wounds
Sohrab. The story ends with the following lines: "This tale is full of
tears, and Rostam leaves / This tender heart indignant as it grieves."
Abolqasem Ferdowsi, *Shahnameh: The Persian Book of Kings*, trans.
Dick Davis. (New York: Penguin Books, 2016), 187-214.

این تناقض عجیبی ست، دل بخواهد و زبان نه
گفتن و نگفتنم چیست؟ چشم آری و دهان نه

این تناقض عجیبی ست بر خلاف کار دنیا
در خیال عشق باشی، در خیال آب و نان نه

این تناقض عجیبی ست، بین بودن و نبودن
زنده ای و زندگی را، هست نامی و نشان نه

لب فشرده ام به تلخی، جان سپرده ام به سختی
تا شبیه خویش باشم تا شبیه این و آن نه

انتظار شرّ و آفت، از زمین و آسمان هست
انتظار خیر و برکت از زمین و آسمان نه

پرسش تو حق من بود، روشن است پاسخ من:
آری، آری، آری، آری می نویسم و بخوان: نه!

꩜

روز و شبم کی رفت؟ کی آمد؟ نفهمیدم
از روز و شب غیر از خطی ممتد نفهمیدم

پرسیدم از خود بارها در خواب و بیداری
از بودنم دنیا چه می خواهد، نفهمیدم

شاید که فرقی بین بودن یا نبودن نیست
یا من چنان که باید و شاید نفهمیدم

Strange contradiction, heart desires, tongue does not
Shall I speak or not? eyes say yes, mouth says not

Strange contradiction, unlike the way of the world
Preoccupied with love, with necessities – not!

Strange contradiction to be or not to be
Alive, yes; living – not!

I have tightened my lips to bitterness, I have endured
    hardships
To resemble only myself, like this person or that one – not!

Expecting evil and disease from the earth and the sky
Expecting good or blessings from the earth and sky – not!

I deserved your question and my answer is clear
Yes, yes, yes, yes I write, and your read it – not!

꙳

My days and nights came and went, I didn't understand
I only knew my days and nights as a long stretch

Awake and asleep, I repeatedly asked myself
What does the world want from me? I didn't understand

Maybe there is no difference between being and not being
Or how I could have and should have, I didn't understand

با چشم و گوشِ بسته راه افتادم و ناچار
شد آن چه شد، باید – نمی باید نفهمیدم

راهی شدم چون و چرایش را نپرسیدم
هیچ از مسیر و مبدأ و مقصد نفهمیدم

آشفته بودم، گیج بودم دور خود هر بار
چرخیدم و هر کس که دورم زد نفهمیدم

با سایه ام هی شعر می خواندم ولی هرگز
می فهمد آیا یاا نمی فهمد نفهمیدم!

دیوانگی های مرا فهمید هر کس دید
بودم...ولی دیوانه تا این حد؟ نفهمیدم

با این دلی که می برد تنها حساب از عشق
ای عقل چیزی از تو صد در صد نفهمیدم

৵

حتی شده یك رشتهٔ نورانی باریك
ای کاش برون آید از این پردهٔ تاریك

ای کاش درآریم سیاه از تن این شب
صبحی برسد غرق گل و بوسه و تبریك

Closed ears and eyes, compelled, I began my journey
What happened, happened, whether it should have or not,
   I didn't understand

I went on my way, no questions asked
Journey, origin, and destination, I didn't understand

Agitated, bewildered, I was going around in circles
All who surrounded me, I didn't understand

I recited poetry to my own shadow
Whether it appreciated it or not, I didn't understand

All who saw me witnessed my madness
I was mad...but to this extent? I didn't understand

With this heart who only fears love
You, my intellect, with certainty, I didn't understand!

❧

I wish even a narrow luminous strand
Could burst forth from this dark curtain

I wish we could take off the night's black cloak
Greet the dawn filled with flowers, kisses and good wishes

تا تاب و تبِ قلب مرا ثبت كنى باز
اى ساعت ديدار بزن تاك بزن تيك

اى دورتر از دورتر از دورتر از دور
نزديك شو نزديك شو نزديك شو نزديك

ॐ

يك عمر اگر دربه در بوده
يا منتظر كسى اگر بوده

با باد اگر به هر طرف رفته
با رود اگر كه همسفر بوده

چون ابر بهار گاه اگر دلتنگ
از لاله اگر شكفته تر بوده

يك چند اگر چو باغ پاييزى
پژمرده و زرد و بى ثمر بوده

خاموش اگر نشسته همچون سنگ
چون آتش اگر كه شعله ور بوده

از پيله اگر نيامده بيرون
از عالم اگر كه بى خبر بوده

To keep pace with the pitter patter of my fervent heart
Sound out, clock, the reunion with your tick and tock

Oh farther and farther and farther than far
Come closer, come closer, come closer, closer

❧

If it were a vagabond all its life...
If it were waiting for someone

If it accompanied the wind all over
If it flowed along with the river

If it were teary eyed like the spring cloud
If it bloomed more open than a tulip

If like an orchard in the fall
It were wilted, yellow and fruitless

If it were silent like a rock
If it were blazing like fire

If it had not left the cocoon
If it were oblivious to the world

در خانه اگر که کودکی شیطان
با اهل محل اگر که شر بوده

دیوانگی اش اگر که گل کرده
انگشت نمای هر گذر بوده

ای عشق فقط تو را تو را می خواست
دل در طلب تو در به در بوده!

ﯜ

به شوق باغ رفتی تشنه و پژمرده بر گشتی
به دریا دل زدی با ماهیان مرده برگشتی

به هر راهی که رفتی راهزن ها در کمین بودند
به هر کس دل سپردی خسته و آزرده برگشتی

سر پُر شورت آخر سنگباران ملامت شد
تو را شیدا فرستادم ولی سرخورده برگشتی

چه قدر آسوده و آرام داری می روی با مرگ
که خیرازِزندگی نادیده و نابرده برگشتی

If it were like a naughty child at home
It it were the prankster of the neighborhood

If its madness had resurfaced
If it were notorious around town

O Love, it only wanted you, wanted you
The heart was a vagabond searching for you!

~

Joyfully, you headed to the garden; parched and wilted you
    returned
You set out for the sea; with dead fish you returned

On each path you chose, thieves were lying in wait
Each time you gave away your heart, hurt and exhausted
    you returned

Your spirited nature became the target of all blame
I sent you out enchanted, but disappointed you returned

How calmly and peacefully you are going along with death
Without seeing or catching a break in life, you returned.

Hila Sedighi

Date of Birth: 1985
Place of Birth: Tehran
Place of Residence: Dubai
Education: BA, Law
Profession: painter, social activist, poet
Books: none

روسری سیاه من

ترس نشسته در دلم، غمزده در نگاه من
سهم من از زنانگی، روسری سیاه من

راز دلم نهان شده، پشت سر حجاب من
غرق گناهم، تو بیا، باز بشو نقاب من

روسری سیاه من سهم من از ستاره ها
دور زحل نشسته ای، در گذر شراره ها

My Black Scarf

Fear settled in my heart, sorrow in my eyes
My share of femininity, my black scarf

Mystery of my heart hidden behind my hijab
I am sinful, come, and become my mask

My black scarf, my share of the stars
Seated around Saturn, sparks flying

تیر نگاه هرزه ها حکم خلاصی که گرفت

نوبت حبس تو و من، زیر گره ها شُل و سفت

روسری سیاه من بخواب روی شانه ام

خمیده پشت من، بیا بدون پشتوانه ام

نقش سپید غصه ها، زده به تار موی من

پود سیاه شو، بیا، بباف آبروی من

نجابت شرقی من قفل تنیده روی لب

بر آفتاب صورتم نشسته سایه های شب

سهم من از زنانگی روسری سیاه من

بپیچ دور گردنم، ببند راه آه من

ترس نشسته در دلم، غمزده در نگاه من

باز بکوب بر سرم، روسری سیاه من

When the gaze of scumbags, piercing as an arrow,
    was acquitted
It's time for you and me to be imprisoned, under
    loose or tight knots

O my black scarf, rest on my shoulder
I am hunched over, come, I have no support

The white pattern of sorrow settled on each strand of
    my hair
Become a black weave, come, save my reputation

My Eastern chastity has locked my lips
On the sunshine of my face shadows of night have
    appeared

My share of femininity, my black scarf
Twist around my neck, close the passage of my sigh

Fear settled in my heart, sorrow in my gaze
Knock me on the head again, O my black scarf!

ای کاش که روحم بگذارد بدنم را
یک سر برود باز ببیند وطنم را
با صبر کسی قفل دری را نشکسته
می‌ترسم ازین آه، بسوزد کفنم را

و

غم نهادینه می‌شود وقتی
گورها جای کافه‌ها پر شد
وقتی از انتشار تاریکی
نور، ماهی و دستمان سر شد
وقتی از کوچه های بی‌لبخند
شیطنت‌های کودکان پربست
هرکس از زندگی مجالی یافت
کار و بار و حسابش آجر شد
روزگار انتقام سختی خواست
از بشر با تمام ابزارش
وقتی روی زمین بخشنده
غارت زندگی تفاخر شد
صف به صف مرده‌های ناخوانده
خط به خط دردهای بی‌مرهم
زندگی بعد از این تراوش مرگ
زیستن نه که یک تظاهر شد

I wish my soul would leave my body behind
To pay a visit to my homeland once again
Nobody's broken a door lock with patience
I fear this sigh, it'll burn my shroud

❧

Sorrow is institutionalized when
Graves, instead of cafés, are filled
When by the spread of darkness
Light became a fish, and our hands slippery
When from joyless alleys
Childish mischief vanished
Whoever caught a break in life
Had his livelihood cut
The world sought a cruel revenge
Against humanity and all its devices
When on this forgiving earth
The looting of life became a badge of honor
Rows and rows of unexpected dead
Layer and layers of intractable pain
Life after the drip drip of death
Not living, merely pretending

Fariba Sedighim

Date of Birth: 1959

Place of Birth: Nahavand

Place of Residence: United States

Education: BS Physical Therapy, Tehran University

Profession: author, poet, editor

Books: two poetry collections

تا مرز نارنج و عصاره ی لیمو

گفتی وقتی قهقهه میزنم

زن میشوم

وتو

تا مرز نارنج و عصاره ی لیمو سفر میکنی

گفتی وقتی زن میشوم

قهقهه میزنم

وتو

روی حریر بدنم

لیز میخوری

تا ته دره های عمیق

To the Edge of the Sour Orange and the Extract of Lemon

You said when I belly laugh
I become a woman
And you
Travel to the border of the sour orange and the
    extract of lemon
You said when I become a woman
I belly laugh
And you
Slide
On my silken body
To the depths of the valleys

گیلاس های خسته

گاه آنقدر نزدیکی
که با اشاره ی انگشت
به قاره ی دیگری پرتاب می شوی
و گاه آنقدر دور
که دست خواب های آشفته ام را می گیری
و به قرارهای سوخته دعوتم می کنی
اتاقی تزیین کرده ام
پر از چشم های خاموش
پر از گیلاس های خسته
تو هرگز به این اتاق پا نخواهی گذاشت
و گلدان های پشت و رو را آب نخواهی داد
تو در قاره های دور می چری
گاه آنقدر نزدیك
که بو سه ام هوا را هدر می دهد
وگاه آنقدر دور
که گر یه ام شانه ات را سنگین می کند
اما
تو هر گز به این اتاق پا نخواهی گذاشت

𒐫

شب بازی اش گرفته با من
پشت هر چیز خودم را پنهان می کنم
تاریکی پیدایم می کند

Tired Glasses

Sometimes you are so close
That by pointing a finger
You are thrown to a different continent
And sometimes so far
That you hold the hands of my disturbing dreams
And you invite me to failed appointments
I have decorated a room
Filled with silent eyes
Filled with tired glasses
You will never set foot in this room
And you will not water the flowerpots, inside or outside.
You graze in distant continents
Sometimes so close
That my kiss wastes the air
And sometimes so far
That my tears weigh down your shoulder
But
You will never set foot in this room!

❧

Night is playing with me
Whatever I hide behind
Darkness finds me

Sarvenaz Seyedi

1979–2009
Place of Birth: Tehran
Place of Residence: [—]
Education: [—]
Profession: artist (painter), author, poet
Books: one poetry collections

می بوسمت
بدون سانسور
و می گذارمت تیتر درشت روزنامه
آن جا که حروفش را
بی پروا چیده اند
خبر هایش را محافظه کارانه
و من همیشه
زندگی را آسان گرفته ام
عشق را سخت.

I kiss you

Without censorship

And I place you as the headline in a newspaper

With its letters arranged fearlessly

Its news cautiously

And I have always taken life easy – love hard.

گمشده

نشانی را گم کرده‌ام
عابری برای سوال نیست
یا پلیسی برای کمك
وصل می‌شوم به اینترنت
و چاقو تیز می‌کنم
برای عشق
در آشپزخانه

Lost

I have lost the address
No passerby to ask
No policeman to help
I connect to the internet
And sharpen the knife
For love
In the kitchen

Nilofar Shidmehr

Date of Birth: 1969

Place of Birth: Tehran

Place of Residence: Canada

Education: PhD in Cross Faculty Inquiry in Education;
  MFA, Creative Writing; BA, Philosophy and Creative
  Writing, all from the University of British Columbia;
  BS, Mechanical Engineering, Khajeh Nasireddin-e Tussi
  University of Technology

Profession: instructor, researcher, essayist, author, translator
  and poet

Books: five poetry collection

درمان دلتنگی

دلتنگ شدی درختی آغوش بگیر
چون شاخه شکوفه‌ای قلمدوش بگیر
با دیدن غنچه‌ها دلت را وا کن
چون برگ نوای نور را گوش بگیر

Treating the Blues

When you feel down, hug a tree
Like the branch, give a blossom a piggyback ride
Look at the budding flowers to cheer up
Like the leaf, listen to the melody of light

سرشار طراوت است هر ذرهٔ خاك
سرشار هوای تازه همچون دل پاك
سرشار چمن، نرگس و آلاله و یاس
سرشار طرب چو آب جوشنده ی تاك

و

Filled with freshness, each bit of soil
Filled with fresh air, like a pure heart
Filled with grass, daffodils, buttercups and jasmine
Filled with joy, like bubbling grape juice

Azadeh Tahaei

Date of Birth: 1967
Place of Birth: [—]
Place of Residence:
Education: [—]
Profession: poet
Books: three poetry collections

آدم‌ها می‌آیند
زندگی می‌کنند
می‌میرند
و می‌روند
اما
فاجعه‌ی زندگی تو
آن هنگام آغاز می‌شود
که آدمی می‌میرد
اما
نمی‌رود
می‌ماند
و نبودنش در بودن تو

People come

Live

Die

Leave

But

The tragedy of your life

Starts when

Someone

Dies

But does not leave

Remains

His absence settles within your being

چنان ته نشین می‌شود
که تو می‌میری در حالی که زنده‌ای
و او زنده می‌شود در حالی که مرده است

از مزار که بازگشتی
قبرستان را به خانه نیاور

❧

یک روز با زندگی قرار گذاشتم
ساده بود:
روزها
سرِ قرار با هم می‌نشستیم
فنجان ـ فنجان
چای می‌نوشیدیم
وُ
بشقاب ـ بشقاب
گپ می‌زدیم
روزی دیگر
خواستم
قرار را به هم بزنم
با زندگی بی‌قرار شوم
نشد!

in such a way
That you die, though you are alive,
And he becomes alive though he is dead

When you return from the grave
Don't bring the graveyard home

꙳

One day, I made a pact with life

It was simple:

Everyday

At our meeting place, we would sit together

And drink tea

Cup after cup

And

We would chat

Plate after plate

Another day

I wanted to break our pact

Have no pact with life

It did not work out

نمی‌شد!
یک کتری
نفرت می‌خواهد
وُ
یک قاشق چایخوری
شهامت
که
ندارم

It couldn't
It needs a kettle
filled with hatred
And
A teaspoon of
courage
That
I do not have.

Parvaneh Vahidmanesh

Date of Birth: 1980
Place of Birth: Tehran
Place of Residence: United States
Education: MA History, Shahid Beheshti University; BA
  History, Tehran University
Profession: human rights activist, broadcaster, poet
Books: one poetry collection

از چشمانم تا چشمانت
چند ایست بازرسی
چند مرز دیگر
چند بار اوراق هویت را باید هویدا کنم؟
از چشمانم تا چشمانت چند چروک دیگر؟
زمین چند دور باید بچرخد؟
چند نفر باید کور شوند تا دوباره تو را ببینم؟
بگو چند چشم از چشمانت تا چشمانم مانده؟

در تبعید....

From my eyes to yours
Several checkpoints
Several other borders
How many times will I have to show my ID?
From my eyes to yours, how many more wrinkles?
How many times does the earth have to rotate?
How many people have to become blind so I can
   see you again?
Tell me how many eyes remain between your eyes
   and mine?

In exile....

این روزها زنی در من راه می رود
از رگهایم عبور می کند
آنقدربالا می رود تا به شقیقه هایم می رسد
از چشمانم طراوش می کند بیرون
گاهی اشك می شود
گاهی نگاه
گاهی لبخند
صبح ها که از خواب بیدار می شوم
او هم بیدار می شود
جلوی آیینه که می ایستم
پشت سرم ایستاده
زل که می زنم در آینه
چروکهای دور چشمهایش را عمیق تر می بینم
دست می کشم روی آینه
دستم را لمس می کند
چای می ریزم
گوشه ای می ایستد و نگاهم می کند
از خانه می زنم بیرون
با من راه می افتد
وقتی می نویسم
مرا می خواند
کنارم می نشیند
زل می زند به اتوبان ها و ماشین ها
حرف نمی زند
گاهی تنها شعری می خواند
با مولانا می رقصد
با فروغ می گرید
با شاملو تصمیم می گیرد
راه می رود
تمام کاشی های خانه را قدم می زند
دخترك را در آغوش می گیرد

These days a woman walks inside me

Passes through my veins

She climbs up and reaches my temples

Seeps out of my eyes

Sometimes in the form of a tear

Sometimes a gaze

Sometimes a smile

In the mornings, when I wake up, she, too, wakes up

When I stand in front of the mirror, she is standing
  behind me

When I stare in the mirror

The wrinkles around her eyes seem deeper

I touch the surface of the mirror

She touches my hand

I pour tea

She stands in a corner and watches me

I leave the house, she leaves with me

When I write, she reads me

She sits next to me and stares at the highways, the cars

She doesn't speak

Sometimes, alone, she recites a poem

Dances with Rumi,

Cries with Forough

Decides with Shamlou

She paces

All the tiles in the house

Hugs the little girl

و آرام می خواند
من و تو آن دو خطیم آری
موازیان به ناچاری
اشک می ریزد
و من تنها
صدای کفشهایش را می شنوم
که درونم ساییده می شود
ساییده می شود
تا به چارچوب در برسد
بعد محو می شود در چارچوب
می رود تا نمی دانم کجا
زنی این روزها در من است
می پزد، می شوید، تمیز می کند، برق می اندازد
بچه ها را بزرگ می کند
و جوانیش را ذره ذره پیرمی شود
پیر می شود و پیر می شود
پیر می شود
و من می ترسم هم اینجا درونم
درون رگها و شقیقه هایم
روی آینه قدی کنار در
بمیرد و من یتیم شوم

And whispers
You and I are, indeed, those two lines,
destined to be parallel
She cries
And I only hear the sound of her shoes
That grate my insides
Grates it until
She reaches the door
And then disappears in the frame
Goes to I don't know where
There is a woman inside me these days
Who cooks, washes, cleans, polishes
Raises the children and
Spends her youth getting old
Getting older and older
And older
And I am afraid
That here, inside me
Inside my veins and temples
In the full length mirror by the door
She would die and I would become an orphan

Pirayeh Yaghmaii

Date of Birth: [—]
Place of Birth:[—]
Place of Residence: Australia
Education: [—]
Profession: poet, translator, author
Books: [—]

آن گاه که

آنگاه که...
پرده را به یک سو کشیدم
و خنکای تُرد
حجم سنگین اتاق را
در خویش گرفت
دریافتم که من و تو
گرگ و میش یک سحرگاهیم
...

༅

The Moment

The moment…
When I pulled the curtain to the side
When the crisp cool air
Enveloped
The heavy air of the room,
I learned that you and I
Are the twilight of a single dawn
…

شبانه

من صدایش را شنیدم

کلاغ بود که قرآن می خواند.
و پرهایش، ادامه شب بود
و
شب آن رودخانه ی جاری بود
که رخت سوگواران را،
در نیل فرو می بُرد.

وهم در آن هنگام بود،
که درد
قلّاده ای
به گردنم می بست

The Crow

I heard its sound.

The crow reciting the Qur'an
And its feathers, the continuation of night

And the night was that flowing river
Dipping the clothes of mourners
In the Nile.

And at that very moment
pain
Was tying a leash
Around my neck

Mandana Zandian

Date of Birth: 1972
Place of Birth: Esfahan
Place of Residence: United States
Education: MD
Profession: physician, author, poet
Books: five poetry collections

كلمات زنده اند
نفس می کشند
خواب می بینند
عشق می ورزند و
مثل درد
در کمرگاه مرگ می پیچند و
جان می دهند و
شعر می شوند و
می مانند...

Words are alive*
They breathe
Dream
Love and
Like pain
They encircle death and
Gradually die and
Become poetry and
Stay…

_____

*This and next 2 poems have also been translated by Ahmad
Karimi-Hakkak.

ما تنها نیستیم؛
پرندگانی سر گردانیم
که از خواب کلمات
نمی پریم.

۵

مثل زن های کولی
دنبال جاده های
بی مقصد می گردم
در گوشه های آغوشت
هوای دریا به سرم زده
و شرجی شانه هایت
و امواج تنت
که بومی تنم شده اند
تو رفته ای
و آفتاب گردان های حاشیه ی دامنم
تا جنوبی ترین رؤیای خدا
قد کشیده اند.

۵

شب ها بدون نام تو می آیند
و نبودنت، دیگر،
جای خالی ات را پرنمی کند
کاش چراغ ماه را خاموش می کردی،
شب را نمی دیدم.

۵

We are not alone;
We are wandering birds
Who will not awaken
From the dream of words.

❧

Like gypsy women
I am looking for roads
With no destination
In the folds of your embrace
I dream of the sea
And your humid shoulders
And the curves of your body
That have become a native part of mine
You have left
And the sunflowers on my skirt's border
Have stretched to
The southernmost dream of God

❧

Nights arrive without your name
And your absence
No longer fills your empty place
I wish you'd turn off the moonlight,
So I wouldn't see the night.

❧

نگران نباش
این پرتگاه هم پنجرهای دارد مثل پاگردِ راهپله
آرام اگر بمانی وُ پلک نزنی
سقوط میکنی در خودت، صبور، وُ
سکوت
زخمهایت را در گلوی گلدانهای کهنه میکارد وُ
یکروز
دوباره در آسمان رها میشوی، سبک
وَ چیزی از تو گرم میکند این
ویرانی را.

❧

صدایت کردم
شعر راه شد
درد راه شد
دلتنگی راه شد
صدایم کرد
راه افتادم
ماه چرخید
راه رود شد
رویید
میوه داد
سرخ شد
دانهام کرد

Don't worry
This cliff too has a window like the landing of
    a staircase
If you stay calm and not blink
You will crash into yourself, patient, and
Silence
will plant your wounds in the depths of old
    flowerpots and
One day
You will be set free in the sky, light,
And some part of you warms up
this ruin

※

I called out your name
Poetry became a path
Pain became a path
Longing became a path
He called out my name
I started on a path
The moon rotated
The path became a river
Grew
Bore fruit
Became red
Seeded me

راهی نبود
برای تاب آوردن
باید به یاد آورد.

؏

چند پاره می‌شود زمان،
چشم که می‌زنی، هر بار، وُ
پروانه می‌شود خیالی
که بافته می‌شود
در دنیایی که تن می‌زند از تثبیت وُ
فرو می‌افتد پرده‌های پی‌درپی‌اش، سنگین وُ
خاطره می‌شود یاد وُ
ثبت می‌شود در سینه‌خیزِ سکوت وُ
سر می‌رود از نور، صدا، تصویر وُ
از پروانه پرواز می‌ماند،
از من، تو
وَ کتیبه‌ای
که می‌داند
تو شادترین سکوت من بوده‌ای

There was no way
to endure
We must remember

Time is torn into many pieces,
When you blink, each time, and
The dream as it's woven
turns into a butterfly
in a world that remains silent and stable, and
its curtains collapse one after the other – heavy, and
Thoughts becomes memories, and
Are registered
in the creep of silence and
It overflows with light, sound and images, and
Of the butterfly flight will remain,
Of me, you
And an epigraph
That knows
You have been my most joyous silence

SELECTED SOURCES

Books

Abedi, Kamyar, ed., *Sad Saal She'r Zanan 1299-1399: Montakhab-e-She'r-e Azad, Nimaii va Sepid* [100 years of women's poetry in Iran 1920-2020: a selection of free verse and prose poems]. Tehran: Morvarid Publication, 2022.

Aghaee, Mana, *Man Issa Ibn-e Khodam* [I Jesus my son]. Stockholm: Alfabet Maxima, 2007.

———. *Zemestan Ma'shoogh-e Man Ast* [Winter is my beloved]. Stockholm: Cypress Bokforlag, 2012.

Amini, Asieh. *Be Khab-e Man ba Tofang Naya* [Don't come in my dream with a gun]. Norway: Communicatio Forlag, 2011.

———. *Baray-e Deltang Shodan Baray-e To Deltang Mishavam* [I miss missing you]. Norway: Communicatio Forlag, 2013.

Azar, Shabnam. *Khoonmahi* [Blood fish]. Cologne: Deed Publishing, 2018.

Bagheri Goldschmidt. *Gol-e-Yakh* [Wintersweet flower]. Nowshahr: Naasang Publishing, 2018.

Bahrami, Razieh. *Noqlha-ye-Koochak-e-Rangi* [Colorful little candies]. Tehran: Daftar-e She'r-e-Javan, 2005.

Chamankar, Roja, *Ramz-e Obur az Balhayam* [The secret of passing through my wings]. Tehran: Negah Publishing, 2021.

———. *Rafteh Budi barayam Kami Jonub Biavary* [You had gone to bring me some of the south]. Tehran: Nim Negah Publishing. 2011.

———. *Labkhoni-e Cheshmhayat* [Reading your eyes]. Tehran: Nimaj Publishing, 2016.

———.*Raah Raftan Ru-ye Band* [Walking on a tightrope]. Tehran: Dalaho Publishing, 2013.

Dastaran, Sareh. *Dolphinha dar Khabhayam Shena Mikonand* [Dolphins are swimming in my dreams]. Tehran: Amoot, 2013.

Farjami, Leila, *Roodkhaneh-ey ke az Maah Migozarad* [The river that goes by the moon]. US: (self-pub., 2011).

———. *Yousefi ke Lab Nazadam* [Joseph I did not taste]. Shiraz: Nashr-e-Kian, 2002.

———. *Zan/Makhroot-e Siah* [Woman/black cone]. Shiraz: Nashr-e Kian, 2000.

Firoozkoohi, *Nikki, Payeez Sad Saaleh Shod* [Autumn turned one hundred years old], Tehran: Maah Baran Publishing, 2013.

———. *Parandehey ke az Baam-e Shoma Parid* [The bird that flew away]. Tehran: Maya Publishing, 2016.

Galehdaran, Leili. *Señor* [Señor]. Stockholm: Nashr-e Baran, 2012.

———. *Yousefi ke Lab Nazadam* [Joseph I did not taste]. Shiraz: Nashr-e-Kian, 2002.

———. *Zan/Makhroot-e Siah* [Woman/black cone]. Shiraz: Nashr-e Kian, 2000.

Habib, Taraneh. *See-o-seh Morgh* [Thirty three Birds] (Tehran: Bedoon, 2022).

Heydari, Zahra. *Doshnomha-ye-Bimokhatab* [Insults without an interlocutor]. Tehran: Anjoman-e-Shaeran-e Iran, 2014.

Hoveyda, Hengameh. *Farar az Pelleh haye Ezterari.* [Escaping through the firescape]. Tehran: Nimaj Publishing, 2013.

Kahrobaeian, Samaneh, *Eltiam* [Healing]. Tehran: Fasl-e-Panjom, 2018.

———. *Vali Beh In Diri* [But so late]. Tehran: Fasl-e-Panjom, 2016.

Kordbacheh, Leila, *Avaz-e Kargadan* [Song of rhinoceros]. Tehran: Nimaj Publishing, 2016.

———. *Meyan-e Jiveh va Anduh* [Between mercury and sorrow]. Tehran, Negah Publishing, 2021.

Mirzaei, Soheila, ed., *Diaspora-ye-She'r: Ba Assari az Shaeran e Zan e Mohajer e Irani* [Diasporic poetry: poetry by Iranian immigrant women]. Norway: Aftab Publication, 2021.

Mossaed, Jila, *Sogand Beh Chehre-ye-Mah* [To the face of the moon]. Kista: Kitab-I-Arzan, 2022.

Nikroo, Sepideh, *Ragbaad* [Ragbaad]. Tehran: Rozaneh Publishing, 2021.

———. *Sofreh-ye Haft Khoon* [Spread of seven bloods]. Tehran: Nashr-e Gooya, 2019.

Nooriala, Partow, *Chahar Rooyesh* [Four growths]. Los Angeles: Sandbaad, 2004.

Salarvand, Fatemeh, *Soosan* [Lili]. Tehran: Neyestan, 2019.

Tahaei, A. *Rooy-e Pol-e- Alma Che Mikonid, Khanoom?* [what are you doing on alma bridge, madam?]. Tehran: Ahang-e-Digar Publishing, 2009.

Other Sources

The rest of the poems have been posted on the poets' pages, Instagram, Facebook or Telegram accounts, have been sent to me by the poet, or were available, on other websites. Most common sites used were Baran Ya'ni to Barmigardi, Adabestan She'er-e Parsi, Sha'er, Shereno, and She'erha-ye Baran Khordeh, Shahrgon, and Shahrvand.